THE NEW RUMANIA

From People's Democracy
to Socialist Republic

CENTER FOR INTERNATIONAL STUDIES
MASSACHUSETTS INSTITUTE OF TECHNOLOGY

Studies in International Communism

THE NEW RUMANIA

From People's Democracy
to Socialist Republic

Stephen Fischer-Galati

THE M.I.T. PRESS
Massachusetts Institute of Technology
Cambridge, Massachusetts, and London, England

FOREWORD

Three of the four major revolts by ruling Communist parties against Soviet authority in the past twenty years—the Yugoslav, Albanian, and Chinese—resulted in at least temporary breaks with Moscow, which have been extensively dealt with in scholarly publications. The fourth, the Rumanian, is the most recent and the most obscure, primarily because it has been only partial and thus deliberately concealed from the public view. Moreover, it is the least thoroughly documented.

The Center for International Studies therefore commissioned two of the leading American specialists in the field, Professors Stephen Fischer-Galati and John Michael Montias, to write a book on this subject. Fortunately, they wrote two: Professor Fischer-Galati on the history and politics of the new Rumania, and Professor Montias on the economics.

Professor Fischer-Galati's volume benefits from his earlier research and publication in Balkan, and specifically in Rumanian, history, his frequent trips to Rumania, the opportunities he has had in Bucharest to discuss problems of Rumanian contemporary history with some of the participants in the drama, and his extensive use of Rumanian sources. I think it fair to say that this study represents the first major revision of contemporary Rumanian history.

Its publication has been made possible by a generous grant by the Ford Foundation to the Institute for research and teaching in international affairs.

Munich, Germany
December 1, 1966

WILLIAM E. GRIFFITH
Director, Project on
International Communism

PREFACE

Rumania, which for nearly twenty years was cited as the most docile of Soviet satellites, as an example of Stalinism triumphant over nationalism, as a country that had lost its past and had no future, has been suddenly hailed as an example of resurgent nationalism, as a symbol of resistance to Kremlin dictates, as a barometer of the international pressures generated by the Sino-Soviet conflict.

The recent assertions of independence—emancipation from Russian tutelage, pursuit of autonomous policies frequently at variance with the rest of the East European states, gradual re-establishment of political, economic, and cultural relations with the West—may seem surprising; but they were not altogether unpredictable. The prevalent conviction, particularly after 1956, that nothing could destroy the monolithic nature of the Soviet bloc resulted in the dismissing as meaningless propaganda of all statements by the current Rumanian leadership. Set forth in the earliest programs of the Rumanian Communist Party were pleas for the attainment of the prescribed social, political, and economic goals; these were interpreted to be admissions of failure by the colorless stooges of Moscow. The purges of such prominent figures as Ana Pauker, Vasile Luca, or Iosif Chișinevski were considered anti-Semitic or anti-Magyar manifestations by a bankrupt leadership seeking scapegoats. Few realized that at least as early as 1955 Gheorghe Gheorghiu-Dej and his associates were cautiously pursuing national policies first formulated in 1945 and envisaging a possible eventual assertion of independence from the Kremlin. This process of internal consolidation and exploitation of external opportunities was sufficiently advanced in April 1964 to allow issuance by the party's Central Committee of the now celebrated *Statement* proclaiming the attainment of the objective conditions for independent action within the framework of general international cooperation. In historic terms, the goals of the Rumanians—the full exploitation of the potential of the Rumanian people and of the country's vast natural resources for the purpose of establishing a respected and prosperous Rumanian state—had been essentially realized. Complete attainment of the national goal would require further socioeconomic progress—toward the ideal Communist society—and, by inference, the recouping of the Rumanian-inhabited territories of Bessarabia and Bukovina from the Soviet Union. The present Rumanian regime thus regards itself as the heir to the historic tradition, as the Communist executor of the nationalist legacy of Greater Rumania.

Although elements of rationalization and propaganda are both evident here, these contentions are basically justified. Rumania in 1966 had indeed realized its "historic legacy" to a much greater extent than at any time in the past. It has solved, often radically, most of the outstanding socioeconomic and political problems that had hampered its development in the twentieth century. The vestiges of the aristocratic-feudal order have been eliminated. The thorny minority problems have been at least alleviated. The industrialization of society has gained momentum. The educational gap between the elite and the masses has been virtually closed. The country's international standing has markedly improved. It is true that many of the solutions—particularly in agriculture—have been inadequate and that numerous problems are still awaiting answers. It may also be argued that the human suffering and sacrifices involved in the attainment of the national Communist goals are not justified in any terms, or that all this and more could have been achieved by means other than those used by the Communist dictatorship, that under the changing world conditions and rapid progress of the industrial revolution in our century the historic legacy would have been truly realized by the democratic forces of the old regime. These and a variety of other arguments, pro-Communist, anti-Communist, neutral, objective, peasantist, liberal, socialist, nationalist, unionist, monarchist, radical, fascist, intuitive, historical, and impressionistic, have glutted the media of public expression for nearly two decades. None, however, has come to grips with the essential question of why Gheorghiu-Dej was able to maintain himself in power for twenty years and preside over the construction of the "New Rumania," despite Russian opposition to the attainment of his goals, and pass on the legacy of independence to his successor, Nicolae Ceauşescu, in 1965.

As the possibilities for investigation of the origins and development of the Rumanian independent course increased in recent years, it became desirable to take stock of all claims and counterclaims, to review and evaluate soberly the extent of Rumania's transformation since 1944 in the light of the historic legacy inherited by the Communists at the end of World War II. This task was undertaken in 1964. It was greatly facilitated by the readiness of Rumanian officials to allow me to conduct research in their country and seek clarification of difficult questions in free discussions. I am profoundly grateful to them for having increased my comprehension of Rumanian problems, even if the views and interpretations contained in this volume are solely my own and, at least in certain instances, at variance with theirs. I am also indebted to American colleagues who provided assistance and advice, particularly to William Griffith, Andrew Gyorgy, John Michael Montias, and Robin Remington as well as to the Center for International Studies and the Ford Foundation for grants in support of the study and to Helen Leek, Mina Parks, Lila T. Rose, and my wife, Anne, for sympathetic encouragement and readying the manuscript for The M.I.T. Press.

STEPHEN FISCHER-GALATI

Boulder, Colorado
October 1966

CONTENTS

THE NEW RUMANIA
From People's Democracy to Socialist Republic

CHAPTER ONE

THE LEGACY OF THE "ANCIEN RÉGIME"

In April 1964 the Rumanian Communist Party issued the celebrated *Statement on the Stand of the Rumanian Workers' Party Concerning the Problems of the International Communist and Working-Class Movement.*[1] The fundamental thesis expounded in that document is the right of all Communist and workers' parties and of the socialist states to "elaborate, choose, or change the forms and methods of socialist construction" in accordance with the "concrete historic conditions prevailing in their own countries. . . ."[2] Given these premises, if one bears "in mind the diversity of the conditions of socialist construction, there are not nor can there be any unique patterns and recipes; no one can decide what is and what is not correct for other countries or parties."[3] Both the justification and explanation for the adoption of the "independent Rumanian course," for the Rumanian rebellion against Soviet dictates and continuous interference in the country's internal affairs, are contained in this key paragraph. Indeed, there can be no meaningful analysis of the process of continuity and change in contemporary Rumania without consideration of the "concrete historic conditions" inherited and altered by the Rumanian Communist Party since the end of World War II.

Paramount in the unenviable legacy of the old regime was the threat of Russian imperialism. This factor *per se* was far more significant than the existence of a state of war between Fascist Rumania and Communist Russia which permitted Russian military intervention in 1944. Even a cursory review of the history of Russo-

---

[1] *Declaraţie cu privire la poziţia Partidului Muncitoresc Romîn în problemele mişcării comuniste şi muncitoreşti internaţionale adoptată de plenara lărgită a C.C. al P.M.R. din aprilie 1964* (Bucharest: Editura Politică, 1964). Revised English translation: William E. Griffith, *Sino-Soviet Relations, 1964–1965* (Cambridge, Mass.: The M.I.T. Press, 1967), pp. 269–296. (Hereinafter in the footnotes it is cited as *Declaraţie.*)

[2] *Declaraţie,* pp. 286–287.

[3] *Ibid.,* p. 286.

Rumanian relations reveals a constant Russian interest in incorporating the Rumanian provinces of Moldavia and Wallachia into the Russian empire or, failing this, exerting political domination over the Rumanian lands.[4] Significant in this context, however, is the fact that Russia's imperialistic designs were, at least until the nineteenth century, frequently endorsed by Rumanian leaders and that friendship with Tsarist Russia was sought and advocated by a considerable segment of the politically conscious population. Rulers like Gheorghe Ştefan or Dimitrie Cantemir, members of the "Russian parties" of the eighteenth century, and even later supporters of political and military alliances with Russia were indeed prepared to accept *de facto* if not *de jure* Russian sovereignty in Moldavia or Wallachia. It is, of course, true that after the revolutions of 1848, particularly the attainment of national independence in 1877 and the establishment of the "Old Kingdom" in 1881, resistance to Russian domination increased among Rumanian politicians. But it would be erroneous to assume that this was an all-prevalent attitude even after the Tsarist annexation of Southern Bessarabia in 1878. The loss of Rumanian territory was naturally opposed by all political parties, but such diverse factors as traditional ties among conservative landed aristocracies, Russian membership in the Triple Entente, and support of Rumanian national aspirations in Transylvania permitted all but the rabid irredentists to overlook the "mutilation of Moldavia" and seek whatever assistance may have been needed for the attainment of their diverse socioeconomic and political goals.

The possibility of cooperation with Russia, however, became remote after the establishment of the Bolshevik order. After World War I the fear of revival of Russian imperialism assumed new dimensions because of Moscow's avowed determination to regain Bessarabia—annexed by Rumania in 1918—and generally to expand the frontiers of communism. The official apprehension even filtered down to the masses, fearful of communism, with the result that Russia was soon regarded as Rumania's main enemy. It is noteworthy, however, that the majority of the population showed little concern over the possibility of recovering Bessarabia other

4 In the absence of any authoritative study of Russo-Rumanian relations the reader is referred to the somewhat superficial, but informative, monographs by Petre Constantinescu-Iaşi, *Relaţiile culturale romîno-ruse din trecut* [The Rumanian-Russian Cultural Relations in the Past] (Bucharest: Editura Academiei, 1954), and Stefan G. Graur, *Les relations entre la Roumanie et l'U.R.S.S. depuis le traité de Versailles* (Paris: A. Pedone, 1936). (Hereafter the latter is referred to as Graur, *Relations.*)

than in the context of the broader Russian Communist threat. If most leaders of the interwar years stressed the dangers of territorial revisionism, it was because their political *raison d'être* was generally equated with the maintenance of the Greater Rumanian state. Unwilling or unable to carry out major programs of socioeconomic reform, conservative politicians from Alexandru Averescu to King Carol II assigned greater priority to the maintenance of the country's territorial integrity than to satisfying the economic demands of the peasantry and working class. Their domestic policies were aimed at circumventing reformist influences, their foreign alignments at containing the revisionists headed by Hungary, Bulgaria, and the Soviet Union.[5]

Whereas the theoretical justification for political inaction failed to appease the dissatisfied, the corollary equating of Russian territorial revisionism with expansion of Bolshevism was more persuasive. With few exceptions the population of Rumania, even if generally disappointed at the policies of venal, incompetent, indecisive, and unrepresentative leaders, opposed Communist solutions to their varying problems. Clearly the land-hungry and downtrodden peasantry rejected the principles of agrarian reform advocated and executed in the Soviet Union. The urban professional classes and bourgeoisie showed no sympathy toward Moscow, and even the industrial workers preferred the indigenous solutions propounded by social democrats to the Russian formulas advanced by the Communists. Only among the oppressed minorities, particularly the Jewish intelligentsia, and the poorer industrial proletariat were supporters of Russia to be found. The constant anti-Russian and anti-Communist propaganda was not lightly dismissed; in fact, it provided the broad rationale for assumption of power by the most virulent exponents of militant nationalism and anti-Bolshevism, the Iron Guard, after the involuntary cession of Bessarabia and Northern Bukovina to Russia in 1940. Thus, paradoxically, those who had invoked the Russian and Communist menace as justification for their regressive policies were either ousted by or joined with the extremists in a common but futile effort to destroy the Soviet Union in alliance with Nazi Germany.

In retrospect, it may well be asked whether the fear of Communist Russia was justified and whether an accommodation would

[5] On these points consult the most comprehensive and sensitive analysis of Rumanian developments in the interwar years, Henry L. Roberts, *Rumania: Political Problems of an Agrarian State* (New Haven: Yale University Press, 1951), pp. 3–222 (hereafter cited as Roberts, *Rumania*).

have been possible. In answering this question it is essential to differentiate between immediate and long-range threats to the territorial and political stability of Greater Rumania. The evidence, scanty as it is, would tend to confirm the generally accepted conclusion that settlement of the outstanding territorial questions would not per se have removed the obstacles to a meaningful accommodation. Bessarabia, in the last analysis, was a political football to the Soviet Union, an instrument for expanding its sphere of influence into southeastern Europe. Whether it sought to intimidate the Rumanian government through the issuance of ultimatums, as in 1919, or the staging of "peasant revolts," as in 1924, or whether it dangled the carrot of peaceful settlement through actual or possible negotiations—as it did in 1924 and 1936—Russia expected far-reaching political concessions as the price of a formal agreement.[6] And this price was always too high for Rumanian negotiators, as it invariably amounted to the establishment of a potential basis for Russian penetration. Ultimately, Russia's true long-range intentions vis-à-vis Rumania were revealed in the discussions related to the determination of spheres of influence in Europe conducted not with the Rumanians but with Rumania's alleged friends or allies in 1939. The reannexation of Bessarabia (enlarged to include Northern Bukovina) demanded from France and Great Britain and agreed to by Germany was necessary to provide a steppingstone for the eventual establishment of a "Russian zone" in Eastern Europe.

On the other hand, the evidence also shows that if Russia's long-range aims were indisputably clear, she did not pose an immediate and direct threat to Rumania in the interwar years either through possible military intervention in Bessarabia or through subversion by the Rumanian Communist Party. The latter is particularly important since the relationship between the Kremlin and the Communist movement in Rumania was a barometer of Russia's intentions and, more immediately, the root cause for Rumania's current independent course. Albeit for different reasons, the policies of Moscow and Bucharest toward the Rumanian Communists coincided in their ultimate aim—the *de facto* liquidation of the party.

Indeed, one of the most significant legacies of the old regime was

---

[6] Graur, *Relations*, pp. 57–157. Ghita Ionescu, *Communism in Rumania 1944–1962* (London: Oxford University Press, 1964), pp. 22–23, 51–52 (hereafter cited as Ionescu, *Communism in Rumania*), provides interesting addenda and corrigenda.

the absence of a viable Communist party.[7] In retrospect, it may be argued that the outlawing of the Rumanian organization in 1924, less than three years after its formal establishment, was a major political error. The party, from its inception, was unrepresentative of the proletariat and enjoyed only minimal support in the factory and village. Its "revolutionary" potential and activities were insignificant, its ties with Moscow weak. The banning of the organization, ordered in retaliation for Russia's refusal to recognize Rumania's rights to Bessarabia, was exploited by Moscow only for propaganda purposes. This Russian attitude cannot be explained only in terms of inability to assist the Rumanian Communists in 1924. Rather it would appear that the Kremlin had already written off the Rumanian organization as an instrument for political revolution in Rumania and had found alternate means for implementing its immediate and long-range goals. Indeed, the history of the Rumanian Communist movement and its relationship with Moscow between 1924 and 1944 reveals a deliberate Russian policy of purging the ever-changing Rumanian Central Committee and of ignoring its political decisions, such as they were.[8]

The reasons for Russia's policies are not difficult to discern. They are ultimately related to Moscow's determination to assign the Rumanian party only an auxiliary role in the attainment of Soviet goals in Eastern Europe. The Russian decision was only partly based on realization that the Rumanian organization did not command the support of the masses. That situation could have been at least somewhat remedied by promoting programs more attractive to the Rumanian peasantry and working class. Even if dogmatism precluded major alterations in Communist theory and practice to con-

---

[7] Regrettably, the history of the Rumanian Communist movement remains obscure. The most comprehensive official survey, Institutul de Istorie a Partidului de pe lîngă C.C. al P.M.R., *Lecţii în ajutorul celor care studiază istoria P.M.R.* [Lessons to Guide Students of the Rumanian Workers' Party History] (Bucharest: Editura Politică, 1960), leaves too many questions unanswered. (Hereafter this is cited as Institutul de Istorie, *Lecţii.*) The several corollary collections of documents, most notably Partidul Comunist din România, *Documente din istoria Partidului Comunist din România* [Documents from the History of the Rumanian Communist Party], 2nd edition (Bucharest: Editura de Stat pentru Literatură Politică, 1953), are too fragmentary to allow the piecing together of a meaningful story. Ionescu's synopsis comprising the introductory chapter to *Communism in Rumania*, pp. 1–68, is most valuable but too brief.

[8] Ionescu, *Communism in Rumania*, pp. 1–34, 41–46. A detailed indictment of Moscow's interference in Rumanian Communist affairs during this period was provided by Nicolae Ceauşescu himself in his speech on the occasion of the Rumanian Communist Party's forty-fifth anniversary on May 7, 1966 (*Scînteia*, May 8, 1966).

form to Rumanian conditions, no such impedimenta can explain Moscow's failure to modify the national and social composition of the Rumanian party's leadership. For it is indeed noteworthy that the party's Central Committee and leading cadres were from the very beginning dominated by Jewish intellectuals and representatives of disaffected national minority groups and that, moreover, only limited efforts were expended on recruitment or promotion of Rumanian workers and "working peasants" into positions of power. A careful study of the Moscow-ordered changes in the party's leadership reveals a constant pattern of replacing defective tools with new or reconditioned Soviet instruments, regardless of Rumanian conditions and reactions. It mattered little to the Kremlin who carried out the functions assigned to the Russian front organization, the Rumanian Communist Party; blind obedience was the only criterion. The conducting of clandestine propaganda among factory workers, penetration of the village, staging of demonstrations, publication of antifascist tracts, and assumption of the role of defenders of peace and democracy apparently required no national or rigid class identification. It is indeed remarkable, and revealing, that a Marcel Pauker or Dobrogeanu-Gherea was succeeded by a Iosif Chişinevski or Vasile Luca; that an Ana Pauker, Boris Ştefanov, Remus Koffler, Iosif Rangheţ, Petre Borilă, or Ştefan Foriş was invariably more trusted and hierarchically above a Nicolae Ceauşescu, Miron Constantinescu, or Alexandru Bîrlădeanu.[9] When taken in conjunction with such factors as the minimal Russian reaction to the bloody repression of the party's greatest achievement, the railway workers' strike of 1933, and indifference for the fate of the leaders of that "Griviţa rebellion," headed by Gheorghiu-Dej, it is possible to reach the conclusion that to Moscow the notion of a viable Rumanian party acting in the interests of the Rumanian masses in accordance with "objective Rumanian conditions" was intolerable even during the interwar years. That this was the case during World War II has been clearly demonstrated by recent documents and public disclosures by the present leaders of the Rumanian Communist Party.[10]

Moscow's attitude toward the Rumanian Communist movement reflected the conviction that replacement of the existing political order was unattainable by Rumanian means alone. Because such

[9] Much insight can be gained from a study of the data contained in Ionescu, *Communism in Rumania*, pp. 40–46 and 350–357, in Institutul de Istorie, *Lecţii*, pp. 289–299, and particularly in *Studii*, XVI, No. 1 (1963), devoted exclusively to the events of 1933.

[10] See in particular Ceauşescu's speech in *Scînteia*, May 8, 1966.

radical political action would have had to be ultimately carried out under Russian auspices, the generalship of the operation had to be entrusted to the Kremlin and its most reliable agents, the non- and anti-Rumanian leaders comprising the so-called "Rumanian bureau" in Moscow.[11] A *de facto* branch of the Russian Communist Party, one of the several foreign groups of that organization, it consisted of the most trusted and servile experts on Rumanian Communist affairs. Throughout the interwar years this Moscow-based and Russian-oriented bureau included at one time or another such "kept women" as Ana Pauker, Boris Ştefanov, Leonte Răutu, Petre Borilă, and others who would be periodically transferred to Bucharest in positions of key responsibility in the Rumanian party. And it was this nucleus, occasionally purified and reinforced, that acted as the "Rumanian general staff" until its wholesale move to Rumania in 1944. The dedicated servants of Moscow lacked identification with Rumania per se. If they advocated social reform, it was primarily to further Russian propaganda rather than Rumanian national ends. This divorcement between social reform and national purpose was indeed detrimental to the cause of the party and was so recognized by at least some of its Rumanian members.

On the basis of still somewhat fragmentary evidence it may be asserted that men like Lucreţiu Pătrăşcanu, the foremost Rumanian member of the Central Committee in the thirties, and Nicolae Ceauşescu and Grigore Preoteasa, significant figures in the Communist youth movement of those years, had more pronounced "domesticist" leanings than the representatives of the Moscow bureau.[12] This was known and exploited for tactical reasons by the Kremlin during the short years of advocacy of antifascist "democratic fronts." It is noteworthy that a considerable segment of the Rumanian intellectual community and the dissatisfied peasantry responded to the patriotic and reformist appeals of these Rumanian Communists with much greater enthusiasm than to those of confirmed agents of the Kremlin. But it is equally significant that no matter how sincere the motivations of these men might have been, their political effort was frustrated. The traditional non-Rumanian personnel and interests of the

11 Ionescu, *Communism in Rumania*, pp. 10, 79–81.
12 Institutul de Istorie, *Lecţii*, pp. 345–361; Al. Gh. Savu, "Folosirea de către, P.C.R. a campaniei alegerilor parlamentare din iunie 1931 în vederea strîngerii legăturilor cu masele" [The Use by the Rumanian Communist Party of the Parliamentary Election Campaign from June 1931 with a View to Strengthening Relations with the Masses], *Studii*, XV, No. 1 (1962), pp. 39–66; Titu Georgescu, "Activitatea comitetului naţional antifascist (1933–1934)" [The Activity of the National Antifascist Committee], *ibid.*, XIV, No. 2 (1961), pp. 323–352.

Communist movement were stressed in discrediting the "new orientation" as a Soviet maneuver. This ammunition, most virulently utilized by the right-wing political parties, virtually destroyed the organization in 1940 when it was put *hors de combat* by the action of its sponsors and the reaction of its fiercest opponents. Ruined by its endorsement of the Hitler-Stalin pact and the seizure of Bessarabia and Northern Bukovina by the Soviet Union, the party was *de facto* dismembered by the Iron Guardist regime. The known leaders of the Rumanian movement, if not already incarcerated, were either jailed or placed under house arrest. The only exceptions were the Bessarabian contingent, the few initiated who were in that province at the time of the annexation, the resident members of the Moscow bureau, and Ana Pauker, exchanged for Corneliu Codreanu's father. The division between the expendable, incapacitated front men and the reliable, reinforced Moscow group was evident on the eve of Rumania's entry into the war on the side of Nazi Germany.

The defeat of the Rumanian organization proved to be a Pyrrhic victory first for its Rumanian and some twenty years later for its Russian opponents as well. The rounding up of the few active members of the illegal organization in 1940 was as symbolic of the failure of the several Rumanian regimes of the interwar period as the banning of the party in 1924. For evidently if the Communist movement per se had but few followers, the need for socioeconomic and political reform—inherent in the misapplied and misinterpreted Marxist doctrine—had been long recognized by the majority of the population of Greater Rumania. The inability of all governments and political parties active between 1918 and 1944 to provide meaningful solutions to the urgent desiderata of the nation provided, on the one hand, the rationale for communism at the end of the Second World War and, on the other, the specific "concrete historic conditions" referred to in the *Statement* of April 1964.

Among the most troublesome elements of the historic legacy left by the old regime were the unresolved agrarian problem, with the corollary mass dissatisfaction of the peasantry, and the nationality question with its ugly anti-Semitic and anti-Hungarian manifestations. Whereas not all political organizations may be equally blamed for their failure to provide satisfactory reform programs, it is evident that none, whether holding office or in opposition, sought to resolve the enormous contradictions and conflicts built into the socioeconomic structure of the Greater Rumanian state. As generally recognized, the principal domestic issue was the peasant.[13] The medieval inheritance of a largely illiterate, "neoserf," Rumanian peasantry may have defied solution even by the most reformist of rulers. Those of Greater Rumania satisfied themselves with implementing the inadequate provisions of the agrarian reform wrested from the monarchy during World War I in a manner essentially detrimental to the peasants' interests. The politicians' reluctance to incorporate the peasantry fully into the country's economic and political life is most readily explained by their determination to prevent the peasant from gaining political power. This attitude, fully comprehensible in terms of the social composition and political philosophy of the leading parties, was at best shortsighted; at worst—given the rulers' inability to satisfy the peasants' economic needs—it exacerbated the traditional, residual antagonisms between town and village, between landlord and serf. Moreover, as they were operating on the premise that Greater Rumania was the creation and possession of the Wallachian and Moldavian aristocracy, its descendants and protégés, and, to a considerably lesser extent, the "unionists" of the newly acquired territories, the Bucharest politicians pursued the retrograde policy of disguising their unwillingness to undertake meaningful socioeconomic reform under the banner of supranationalism. Thus not only was the "underdeveloped" Rumanian peasant neglected but also the more advanced Hungarian or Saxon agriculturist was abused.

It is true that the agrarian crisis which tormented Rumania in the thirties was not due wholly to the inadequacies of domestic policies. It is also true that the peasantry's preferred solutions to their economic difficulties, centering on acquisition of additional land, were more often than not unsound and unrealizable in terms of the country's general economic requirements and orientation. However, the deliberate political isolation of the peasantry, failure to improve agricultural techniques, maintenance of backward social and cultural standards, in short the crass neglect of the village, were not conducive to winning the allegiance of the masses or modernizing the socioeconomic structure of the country. The antirural policies and programs of the interwar years were not a monopoly of the Communist, social democratic, conservative, and other political organizations favoring accentuation of industrial development or maintenance of large latifundia. To a lesser degree even the

---

[13] On the Rumanian agrarian problem and its political aspects consult Roberts, *Rumania*, pp. 89–222.

alleged friends or representatives of the peasant, the National Liberal and the National Peasant parties, did relatively little to improve the status of the Rumanian masses during their respective turns in office. Under the circumstances the two major political organizations gradually lost the confidence of the peasant, who turned more and more toward the monarchy or exponents of radical reform programs. In the thirties King Carol II, the Iron Guard, and even the Plowmen's Front were effectively competing with the National Peasant Party for the allegiance of the masses.

Dissatisfaction, in the interwar period, was not limited to the rural population; it was also prevalent in the city. The root cause for this phenomenon was the irrational exploitation of the country's vast economic resources by those in power. True to their philosophy that Greater Rumania was the patrimonial estate of its architects, the Bucharest "power elite," particularly that congregating in the dominant National Liberal Party, pursued a policy of milking the country and dividing the spoils for its immediate benefit.[14] In the twenties the Brătianu family, their industrialist and financial friends, the top echelons of the bureaucracy, and a large retinue of lesser relatives, acquaintances, and officials were jealously guarding and selfishly devouring the national nest egg. The related discriminatory treatment of Hungarian and Jewish commercial, financial, and industrial interests and protectionist trade policies— justified in terms of Rumanian supremacy and national interest— stymied economic progress. The industrial workers were treated shoddily as were the rank and file of the state and private bureaucracy. The Liberals' policies and practices, deplored by the population at large, were also vociferously condemned by an unusually large number of rival political parties. Regrettably, most political organizations had no reformist tendencies; their paramount aim was replacing the National Liberals before the well ran dry.[15] To attain this goal a multitude of theoretical reform programs were propounded; all except those of the Communists, social democrats, and certain peasant organizations emphasized the preservation of national territorial integrity and development of Rumania

14 *Ibid.*, pp. 94–129. An excellent brief discussion of Rumanian political problems and mores in the interwar years is contained in Hugh Seton-Watson, *Eastern Europe Between the Wars, 1918–1941,* 3rd edition (New York: Archon Books, 1962), pp. 198–216.

15 The official programs and doctrines of the various political parties are conveniently summarized in International Reference Library, *Politics and Political Parties in Rumania* (London: International Reference Library Publishing Company, 1936).

for the Rumanians. Moreover, few parties were above compromise with the opposition or the monarchy, since even half a loaf was better than none. In this deplorable political climate little could be achieved, and excesses became inevitable particularly after the start of the world depression. As the competition for the ever more meager spoils increased, so did popular dissatisfaction and corollary political adventurism and right-wing radicalism.

In any mass indictment of Rumanian political parties and of the prevalent political prostitution, several exceptions must be made. Except for minor political groupings, offshoots of the National Liberal and National Peasant parties, which displayed a modicum of political integrity, and except for the social democrats and Communists, all were in one form or another either guilty of collusion with the monarchy, with fascist or protofascist organizations, or of forgoing political promises and reformist principles upon assumption of power. The National Liberals, who dominated the political scene during the interwar years, were hardly above reproach. First under the Brătianu dynasty, later under Gheorghe Tătărescu, they neglected the public interest and undertook virtually no reforms. More significantly, perhaps, they were the initiators of the doctrines related to national supremacy and self-sufficiency which were perpetrated in more virulent forms by the right-wing opposition. Yet, being the party of the Rumanian bourgeoisie and former latifundiaries, it never engaged in the irrational and politically fatal behavior of the extremists. Nor is it possible to exonerate the National Peasant Party for its abysmal failure in the interwar years.[16] As the organization of the peasantry, of the urban reformist intelligentsia and professional classes, of the national minorities seeking equality of rights, of the majority of those opposed to the National Liberals, it held out—in the twenties and thirties—the greatest hope for reform in Rumania. But during its turn in power between 1928 and 1931 it disappointed most of its supporters by pursuing policies not dissimilar to those of its predecessors. With allowances made for such formidable factors as the international economic crisis and royal interference, the socioeconomic and political reform programs advocated by the party's "left-wing" "peasant" contingent were severely circumscribed by the conservative "national" wing led by Iuliu Maniu. Reformism could never transcend the "national interest" framework imposed by Maniu, and this deficiency led to the further

---

[16] For a judicious appraisal of the National Peasant Party's ideology and policies consult Roberts, *Rumania*, pp. 130–169.

weakening of the organization after Maniu's falling out with King Carol II and subsequent conclusion of the much-criticized electoral pact with the Iron Guard in 1937.

The ranks of the disappointed and discontented grew after the National Peasants' failure to fulfill the expectations of their supporters, and the dissatisfaction and cries for reform were not silenced by the Tătărescu regime that followed. Under these conditions the true exponent of national extremism, the fascist Iron Guard, offered its program for "national reconstruction."

Rumanian fascism cannot be explained in terms of the anti-Semitic and anti-Communist tradition alone; indeed, it is comprehensible only as a nationalist social reform movement.[17] Anti-Semitism was fundamental to the doctrine of the Iron Guard. But this inheritance from its parent organization, the League of National Christian Defense, could not per se account for the widespread support enjoyed by the Legionaries in the thirties. The appeal of the Iron Guard ultimately rested in its providing the peasantry, urban proletariat, intellectuals, businessmen, and industrialists with an apparent solution to their problems within an acceptable ideological framework. Conditioned by constant bombardment with chauvinist, anti-Semitic, anti-Communist, anti-Russian, and anti-Hungarian propaganda by most political organizations and the press, a substantial segment of the Rumanian population, frustrated by the failures of "traditional" political parties, was prepared to join the reformist crusade advocated by Corneliu Zelea Codreanu and his followers. In general, apart from the industrialists, businessmen, intellectuals, civil and military servants who were banking or gambling on Hitler's victory, the supporters of the Guardist organization regarded the Legionaries not as agents of Nazi Germany but as Rumanian patriots bent on satisfying their socioeconomic needs. It is difficult to determine the depth of the Guardist roots in the country at large before the downfall of King Carol in 1940, since the monarchy had sought to provide a comparable reform program in the late thirties. But it is clear that the Guard had a substantial following from as early as 1937, as evi-

---

17 Codreanu's own writings, contained in Corneliu Z. Codreanu, *Pentru Legionari* [For the Iron Guard] (Bucharest: "Totul pentru Ţară" [All for the Fatherland], 1937), should be read in conjunction with Roberts, *Rumania*, pp. 223–241, Lucreţiu Pătrăşcanu, *Sous Trois Dictatures* (Paris: Vitiano, 1946), pp. 277–326, and Eugen Weber, "Romania," in Hans Rogger and Eugen Weber, eds., *The European Right* (Berkeley, Calif.: University of California Press, 1965), pp. 501–574.

denced in that year's elections, and did enjoy broad support at the time it drove King Carol into exile in the summer of 1940. It is also noteworthy that even after the removal of the Legionaries from power by Marshal Ion Antonescu, early in 1941, the repudiation of the Guardist methods did not necessarily mean abandonment of their ideology or program. In fact, both doctrine and program were perpetrated under Antonescu's fascist regime with a remarkable degree of success.

In its simplest terms the Iron Guard advocated the removal of all corrupt politicians, destruction of the economic power of the Jews and redistribution of their assets among the Rumanian population, broad land reform, rational utilization of the country's vast economic resources, and a crusade against Rumania's mortal enemy, Communist Russia—the friend and protector of Jews and other national groups inimical to Rumanian interests—in alliance with Nazi Germany. It is true that not all members, followers, or sympathizers subscribed to all aspects of this program. Thus the peasantry was far more concerned with agrarian reform than with anti-Russian crusades. The intellectuals were generally interested in the political reform program and the chauvinistic aspects of the doctrine without subscribing to the pro-German orientation of the movement. Only a hard but influential core of the oppressed proletariat, younger peasants, underpaid civil servants, commissioned and noncommissioned army officers, and high school and university students, with wide contacts in the village, endorsed the most radical aspects of the "Christian crusade" propounded by the Guardist high command.

This does not mean that the majority of the Rumanian people were devoted fascists in the thirties and early forties; but it is evident that, whether fully understood or not, fascism was the most acceptable of the alternatives presented to the dissatisfied Rumanians in those years. The other choices, besides those offered by the major political parties prior to their suppression by King Carol in 1938, were royal dictatorship or one or another form of socialism.

Superficially there was little to choose between the dictatorships of King Carol and the fascists, but in reality the differences were profound.[18] Although the King had been a contributing factor to political immorality and more directly concerned with his personal enrichment and that of his entourage since coronation in 1930, he cannot be held responsible for destruction of the democratic politi-

[18] On the royal dictatorship, its nature and purposes, see Roberts, *Rumania,* pp. 206–222, and Pǎtrǎşcanu, *Sous Trois Dictatures,* pp. 21–231.

cal process or for the country's economic plight any more than most party politicians. That he provided no moral leadership nor actively sought the improvement of political practices is unquestionable. But even though he failed to set standards above those current in interwar Rumania and was unwilling to emulate contemporary Western constitutional monarchs, thus demeaning the royal office, still his actions were so much in keeping with Rumanian political mores that singling him out for blame is not historically justifiable. In fact, the King, by virtue of his position, became a constructive force in political life and did so—to be sure, belatedly—at a time of extreme economic and political difficulties. The effectiveness of his "monarcho-fascist" regime, set up to provide a united political front to cope with the country's socioeconomic problems and the threat of unadulterated fascism, domestic and foreign, can best be measured by the determination of the Iron Guard and Hitler to remove him from power. His proposed agricultural reforms, modest though they were, enjoyed a definite degree of popularity in the villages. His precarious attempts to balance German influence against the traditional French and thus ultimately to ensure Rumania's neutrality were welcomed by much of the Francophile intellectual and professional community. Ultimately, all those fearful of pure fascism were among his supporters. It is true, however, that the support given Carol was more in the nature of a choice between two evils. And it is precisely because of the contradictions inherent in the royal dictatorship that the true fascists were able to overthrow him without risking meaningful popular reaction. It is, however, important that the institution of the monarchy as such was preserved in 1940 not only because it was traditional, historically associated with Greater Rumania, and generally desired by the peasantry but also because Carol's successor, King Michael, endorsed the fascist program and was accepted by the majority of the Rumanians as the honorary leader of a palatable, if not ideal, program of political action and socioeconomic reform.

In contrast, the socialist alternatives presented to the dissatisfied in the thirties were largely theoretical. The social democrats had a respectable following among the working class, but the size of the proletariat was small.[19] The number of intellectuals who were sympathetic to socialist programs may have been fairly large, but as

[19] The most authoritative statement on the social democratic movement in Rumania is by C. Titel Petrescu, *Istoria Socialismului în România* [The History of Socialism in Rumania] (Bucharest: "Cugetarea," 1944).

the Social Democratic Party had virtually no support from the peasantry and nationalists—and consequently was unable to gain political power at the polls—actual identification was nominal. The fate of the Communists, as described, was even worse. However, the Transylvanian Plowmen's Front, a pro-Communist splinter group of the National Peasant Party and member of the Communist-dominated Popular Front of the mid-thirties, attracted a surprisingly sizable following in those years. The land reform program, based on principles of equalitarian distribution and peaceful cooperation among peasants regardless of nationality, was particularly popular in Northern Transylvania, as evidenced by the electoral results of 1936.[20] Still it is most doubtful that, even if it had been permitted to continue its activities, the Plowmen's Front could have effectively competed with the fascists or even with King Carol for the allegiance of the masses. The Vienna *Diktat* of the summer of 1940, assigning Northern Transylvania to Hungary, cut the ground from under the Plowmen's Front as much as the restitution of Bessarabia had ruined its Communist allies. And as both factors had also been most instrumental in the removal of King Carol, the fascists were free to cope with the country's problems all by themselves.

A re-evaluation of the fascist period, particularly under Antonescu, would indicate that its achievements have been generally minimized and that the extent of its rejection by the population has been grossly exaggerated.[21] Antonescu was both an efficient and enlightened dictator compared to his European counterparts of World War II. His reformist measures in agriculture and industry—though they were inspired largely by military necessities—were effective and held out the prospect of further improvement at the war's end. The anti-Russian crusade, at least through the stage of reconquest of Bessarabia and Northern Bukovina, was endorsed by the political leaders of the "traditional parties," including the National Liberal and National Peasant, and generally met with mass approval. Only as defeat became apparent, as the losses of manpower reached unexpected heights, as the country's economic gains were erased because of excessive military demands, German pilferage, and Allied bombings did the base of his support shrink. Nevertheless, even in defeat Rumanian fascism, in its reformist and

<hr>

[20] Institutul de Istorie, *Lecţii*, pp. 362–370.
[21] In this connection see Andreas Hillgruber, *Hitler, König Carol und Marschall Antonescu; Die deutsch-rumänischen Beziehungen 1938–1944*, 2nd ed. (Wiesbaden; Franz Steiner, 1965), pp. 89–235.

extreme nationalist aspects, was not dead. And as politicians began to desert the sinking ship after Stalingrad, they did not necessarily change their views or habits concurrently with their affiliations. To all but the social democrats, "progressive" peasant organizations, and certain survivors of the decimated Communist movement, nationalism and anticommunism remained the ideological framework for any immediate and long-range alteration of Rumania's political and socioeconomic patterns and orientation. The masses shared at least one of the politicians' apprehensions—fear of Communist Russia. Thus, in the troubled days of military withdrawal from the Soviet Union and simultaneously the rapid advance of the Russian forces toward Rumania's borders, a variety of solutions and compromises were being sought by those who at one time or another had been in Antonescu's camp—except by the Marshal himself—all based on the realization that the national, or nationalist, tradition was in grave jeopardy. It was in these chaotic moments that the Rumanian Communists were summoned to political action by Rumanian political figures and by Moscow. The Communists' task was a thankless one.

CHAPTER TWO

THE EMERGENCE OF GHEORGHIU-DEJ (1944–1952)

When in 1963 the diagnosticians of polycentrism discovered the Rumanian case, they reported as one of its symptoms the controversy between Rumanian and Soviet historians on "Rumania's liberation from fascism" in 1944. Interpreted as another manifestation of Rumanian nationalism designed to lessen the country's debt of gratitude to Russia and to drape the mantle of liberators upon the shoulders of the Communist leadership, the "academic" dispute was considered closed upon apparent Russian acceptance of the Rumanian corrigenda.[1] However, the issue of whether the Russian armies "liberated" Rumania or merely supported the "military antifascist insurrection sparked and conducted by the Rumanian Communist Party"—of whether the victorious native revolutionary armies "liberated" Rumania alongside Russian troops—is of cardinal importance to a correct understanding of Russo-Rumanian relations and the corollary Rumanian independent course. For clearly different rights are accrued by "liberators" and "liberated," by victorious nations and defeated nations, by vanquished and cobelligerents. Since Russia's rights and privileges in postwar Rumania were justified by her having conquered the fascist enemy and "liberated" the Rumanian people from that yoke, reparations were extracted on the same principle, and the "democratic" reorganization of the country was claimed as the right of victors—in sum, since the Soviets insisted that "to the victors belong the spoils," the entire range of questions connected with the responsibility for and rights derived from the removal of Antonescu's dictatorship are crucial, at least from a theoretical standpoint.

However, the Rumanian Communist rulers would hardly have raised such questions in 1963, or for that matter much earlier, had it not been for the essential fact that they themselves barely escaped

---

[1] A succinct summary of the problem as seen in 1963 may be found in *East Europe*, Vol. XII, No. 3 (March 1963), p. 51.

"liberation" by the Russians in 1944 and that then, and in ensuing years, the Russians claimed and frequently exercised victors' rights with respect not only to Rumania but also to the leadership of the Rumanian Communist Party that allegedly organized and led the successful "military antifascist insurrection." In short, the struggle for political survival by the authors of the independent course was directly and immediately linked with Russia's interference in Rumanian affairs, by virtue of legal rights vested in the Soviet Union as Rumania's "liberator," and the extralegal ones that the Russian Communist Party had so successfully exercised in its relations with the Rumanian Communist movement in the twenties and thirties. By the same token, the Rumanian Communists' mandate to transform the political and socioeconomic order in their own country is theoretically also derived from their "liberating" Rumania in 1944, from their own victors' rights in Rumania proper. Thus the dispute transcends the limits of interparty or international polemics; given its far-reaching implications, one must ascertain its merits and the validity of the respective positions.[2]

According to sources made available by the Rumanian Communist Party itself, it would appear that from the moment the Rumanian leadership was reorganized in April 1944 and summoned to political action it was faced with the very problems that were to plague it for years to come: political survival and formulation and implementation of plans for the socialist transformation of Rumania. The circumstances surrounding the events of April 1944, particularly Gheorghiu-Dej's release from prison, remain somewhat obscure. The official Communist version that the escape was achieved through the independent efforts of a few dedicated party members headed by Emil Bodnăraş and Ion Gheorghe Maurer is

2 The significance attached by the Rumanians to the party's role in the preparation and execution of the "liberation" is evidenced by the publication of numerous monographs and collections of articles on that very subject. Most noteworthy are *23 August 1944: Culegere de articole* [Collected Articles] (Bucharest: Editura Politică, 1964), hereafter cited as *23 August 1944; Contribuţia României la victoria asupra fascismului* [Rumania's Contribution to Victory over Fascism] (Bucharest: Editura Politică, 1965), hereafter cited as *Contribuţia;* Ion Popescu-Puţuri *et al., La Roumanie pendant la deuxième guerre mondiale* (Bucharest: Éditions de l'Académie de la République Populaire Roumaine, 1964); and A. Petric and Gh. Ţuţui, *L'instauration et la consolidation du régime démocratique populaire en Roumanie* (Bucharest: Éditions de l'Académie de la République Populaire Roumaine, 1964), hereafter cited as Petric and Ţuţui, *L'instauration.*

open to question.[3] Instead it would appear that Bodnăraş, who had been active in the Russian army during the war, had acted on orders from Moscow in connection with a rather intricate mission. The dispatching of Bodnăraş to Rumania was predicated on the realization of two alternate plans devised by the Kremlin: the first, and preferred, plan was to obtain Antonescu's surrender prior to the arrival of the Russian troops; the second was the "liberation" of Rumania by the Russian armed forces. In any event, the fate of Rumania was to be decided independently of whatever plans might have been devised by the Rumanian Communists, whether by the free Lucreţiu Pătrăşcanu or Iosif Ranghet or the imprisoned Gheorghe Gheorghiu-Dej, Gheorghe Apostol, Chivu Stoica, Miron Constantinescu, Alexandru Moghioroş, or Nicolae Ceauşescu.[4] The Kremlin's position was generally known to the politically initiated at least since the fall of 1943, when the first Russian feelers were made with a view to obtaining Rumania's surrender. Informal discussions between Russian officials and foreign representatives of the Antonescu regime were conducted to that end from as early as January 1944. The Russian policy was not motivated as much by military as by political considerations. Determined to acquire control of Rumania, Moscow was fearful that parallel conversations held in Cairo between other emissaries of the Antonescu regime and the British and Americans could lead to the precipitous surrender of the Rumanians to the Western allies, which would have

---

[3] Ion Vinte, "Partidul Comunist din România in fruntea luptei pentru răsturnarea dictaturii fasciste" [The Rumanian Communist Party Leader of the Struggle for the Overthrow of the Fascist Dictatorship], *Scînteia*, July 31, 1964; Constantin Pîrvulescu, "Unitatea de acţiune a clasei muncitoare—un factor esenţial al victoriei insurecţiei din august 1944" [The Unity of Action of the Working Class, an Essential Factor in the Victory of the August 1944 Insurrection], *ibid.*, August 6, 1964. See also Ion Popescue-Puţuri *et al.*, "Insurecţia armată antifascistă din august 1944 şi participarea României la înfrîngerea Germaniei hitleriste: Insemnătatea lor la istoria poporului român" [The Armed Insurrection from August 1944 and Rumania's Participation in the Defeat of Nazi Germany: Its Meaning in the History of the Rumanian People], *Contribuţia României*, pp. 9–34, based on important archival materials. The most explicit account of the escape itself is by Mihai Roşianu, "Cum a fost organizată evadarea tovarăşului Gheorghe Gheorghiu-Dej din lagărul de la Tîrgu-Jiu în august 1944" [How Gheorghe Gheorghiu-Dej's Escape from the Tîrgu-Jiu Camp in August 1944 Was Carried Out], *Scînteia*, August 18, 1964.

[4] Apart from the references given in footnote 3, consult Gheorghiu-Dej's lengthy report to the plenary session of the Central Committee of November 30–December 5, 1961, *Scînteia*, December 7, 1961. Supplementary information is also contained in Ghita Ionescu, *Communism in Rumania 1944–1962* (London: Oxford University Press, 1964), pp. 74–81.

jeopardized its scheme to use Antonescu's surrender as justification for setting up a government of occupation of its own making and choice.[5]

The Russian aims were understood by Antonescu as well as by the leaders of the "traditional" parties. While the former was opposed to any deals with any of the Allies, the latter actively supported first negotiations with the Americans and British and then, with Russian forces rapidly approaching, the staging of an internal coup d'état, establishment of a coalition government, and, following a reversal of alliances, Rumanian assumption of the role of cobelligerent. This multiple maneuver was evidently designed to frustrate Russia's plans for Rumania. The leaders of the non-collaborationist parties were also approached by Maniu and other plotters on the correct assumption that the Russians would not tolerate an unrepresentative government upon reaching Rumania. Faced with this situation in the early spring of 1944, the free Rumanian Communist leaders, acting through Lucreţiu Pătrăşcanu, decided to endorse the coup against Antonescu and to enter a coalition government upon the Marshal's removal from power.[6]

Bodnăraş's mission was apparently designed to delay implementation of these plans by first seeking Antonescu's surrender or, failing in this, directing Rumanian Communist activities preparatory to the Russians' arrival. Unable to make much headway in its negotiations with Antonescu, Moscow soon consented to the freeing of the jailed leaders of the party on the assumption that they would readily follow orders. What Russia ignored was the extent of the independent political activity of the jailed and their awareness of the Kremlin's intentions. Even without giving total credence to the current Rumanian version of Gheorghiu-Dej's team mapping today's political plans while incarcerated, the evidence is at least conclusive with respect to his and his associates' opposition to any compromise with Antonescu and their readiness to participate in any action that would overthrow the fascist regime and bring Rumania to the side of the Allies. It is also clear that these men were convinced of the inevitable establishment of a Communist regime in Rumania at the end of the war with Russian assistance and under Russian supervision. What has not been so evident until

---

5 F. C. Nano, "The First Soviet Double-Cross," *Journal of Central European Affairs*, Vol. XII, No. 3 (1952), pp. 236–258, and Alexandre Cretzianu, *Lost Opportunity* (London: J. Cape, 1957), pp. 123–149, provide interesting data on these problems.

6 *23 August 1944*, pp. 3–71.

the releasing of materials on the events of 1944 was the divergence between their program and the Russians' and their suspicions of the Soviet Union.[7]

It is indeed noteworthy that on the eve of Gheorghiu-Dej's liberation the leaders present at the *ad hoc* "plenary" meeting held in the prison infirmary, including Bodnăraş, Gheorghiu-Dej, and Chivu Stoica, approved two crucial steps: the purging of Foriş, the party's First Secretary, and the continuation of negotiations with the traditional parties along the lines pursued by Pătrăşcanu.[8] Both actions may be considered as contrary to Russian policies. Foriş's removal is particularly significant since he had entertained contacts with the Antonescu regime, with Moscow's approval, at least since the fall of 1943. From the thinly disguised references to his crimes it may be gathered that the Russian offer for a deal with Antonescu included the sacrificing of a then expendable Rumanian Communist organization. Aware of Russian political cynicism from their interwar and wartime experience, the imprisoned Rumanian Communists had seemingly decided to seize control of the Rumanian party and solidify their own position prior to the arrival of the Russian armies and Moscow's Rumanian bureau. The expulsion of Foriş from the post of First Secretary and his replacement by Gheorghiu-Dej at the meeting of April 4, 1944 and the new leaders' decision to participate in collective political action with "bourgeois" organizations were indicative of their intention to gain a potentially dominant position in the country's political life, which the Russians would have to accept if not necessarily approve.[9]

The April decisions were not made hastily. Gheorghiu-Dej was far too careful a person even then to leave his tracks uncovered. Disregarding Russia's preferences, he, as well as Bodnăraş, banked on the inevitability of a coalition government, given Antonescu's intransigence and the activities of the traditional political parties. During a transitional period of "Popular Front" rule, individuals with roots in the Rumanian working-class movement would be indispensable and hence acceptable to Moscow. Nevertheless, considering the outside possibility of a last-minute deal between Antonescu and Stalin or any other unexpected change in the po-

---

[7] See footnote 3.

[8] Vinte, "Partidul comunist," *op. cit.,* and Pîrvulescu, "Unitatea," *op. cit.*

[9] See in particular Roşianu, "Evadarea," *op. cit.,* providing the most detailed information on the meeting of April 1944. For related materials in all publications see footnote 3.

litical situation, Gheorghiu-Dej, Bodnăraş, and their associates decided to remain in the background, leaving Pătrăşcanu, an intellectual, to assume the risks inherent in negotiations with the "bourgeois" parties.[10]

The events immediately following the prison meeting and Gheorghiu-Dej's escape tend to confirm this interpretation. It was Pătrăşcanu who negotiated the establishment of the United Workers' Front with the Social Democratic Party in April 1944 and of the People's Democratic Front, including the National Peasant, National Liberal, Social Democratic, and Communist parties, in May, while Bodnăraş and Gheorghiu-Dej were concentrating on the recruiting of new members and consolidation of ties with the Hungarian workers' organization MADOSZ, the Plowmen's Front, and other left-wing groups comprising the Anti-Hitlerist Patriotic Front set up by the Communists in the summer of 1943. The extent to which they were concurrently organizing the "military insurrection" is by no means clear. That Bodnăraş was a participant in a meeting with General Sănătescu, the head of the coalition government established after the coup of August 23, and other military and political leaders in June is confirmed by the evidence. It is also known that a plan to stage a military coup against Antonescu before the arrival of the Russian troops in Bucharest was drawn up at that time. However, the initiative and subsequent preparations were the extent of the collective undertaking, and on August 23 the coup itself was staged without the knowledge of the Communists.[11]

It is certain that King Michael's order to arrest Antonescu on August 23 was issued on the recommendation of Maniu, General Constantin Sănătescu, and other non- or anti-Communist members of the conspiracy. Antonescu's decision—communicated to the monarch that very day—to accept the previously rejected Russian proposals for surrender would have been catastrophic for the representatives of the traditional parties seeking to establish a coalition government and to shift alliances without acknowledging military

10 That Pătrăşcanu was singled out as a potential sacrificial lamb is clear from the cooptation of Constantin Pârvulescu and Iosif Rangheţ—two of his closest proletarian associates—into the revamped leadership on April 4, 1944.

11 Pîrvulescu, "Unitatea," op. cit.; Dumitru Simulescu, "Formaţiunile de luptă patriotice în insurecţia populară antifascistă," Scînteia, August 12, 1964; Dumitru Dămăceanu," Pregătirea militară a insurecţiei armate subconducerea partidului Comunist din România," ibid., August 9, 1964; and Contribuţia, pp. 19–66.

defeat. The Communists were informed, ex post facto, of Antonescu's arrest, the establishment of a government headed by Sănătescu, and the royal proclamation of Rumania's joining the Allies in the common struggle against Nazi Germany.[12] What the response of the party's leadership would have been had it been appraised by the King of Antonescu's decision is a matter of speculation. On the basis of the evidence previously analyzed, it may be surmised that even if not spared the dilemma, Gheorghiu-Dej and his associates would have agreed, as they did when faced with the *fait accompli,* to the inclusion of Pătrăşcanu in the Sănătescu regime and support of the military operations directed against the German forces stationed in Rumania. To this extent, then, the claims of the Rumanian Communists regarding their role in their country's liberation have some validity. While certainly not the sole moving force behind the conspiracy or during the military actions preliminary to the Russian armies' entering Bucharest on August 30, they had committed themselves to participation in a common Rumanian effort with all the risks inherent in incurring the Kremlin's wrath.

However, one must never lose sight of the fact that no matter how contrary to Russia's interests their actions may have been, the leaders of the party did not regard their differences with Russia as irreconcilable. Ultimately, these differences centered on the role of the Rumanian contingent in the process of transformation of Rumania into a socialist state. A study of the writings and records of Gheorghiu-Dej, Bodnăraş, Ceauşescu, Apostol, and their closest associates leaves no doubt that these men were as determined as the Russians, in August 1944, to sabotage the coalition government and to bring about its rapid downfall. Moreover, there was agreement on tactics vis-à-vis the Western allies. The Rumanians were also ready to accept the incorporation into the party's Central Committee of members of the Moscow group and general guidance of the party's activities by the Russians. On the other hand, they expected to play a decisive role in the formulation of internal strategy, policy, and planning—based on their appreciation of domestic conditions—and to retain control of the party apparatus. In short, then, on the eve of the Russians' entry into Bucharest the Ruma-

---

[12] The carefully documented analysis by Ionescu, *Communism in Rumania,* pp. 83–86, is corroborated by later evidence contained in *23 August 1944,* pp. 3–65, 72–80, and 102–105.

nian contingent was ready to embrace the Russian brethren as cobelligerents, coliberators, and advisors in the preparation and execution of the inevitable political and social revolution.[13]

The Russians, however, immediately dispelled whatever illusions the Rumanians might have entertained. The concepts of cobelligerency and coliberation were rejected outright; the Rumanian troops siding with the Red armies were recognized only as "collaborators." Communist participation in the Sănătescu cabinet was condemned and the principal blame assigned to Pătrăşcanu as one of the architects of the coalition and the party's representative in the government. Gheorghiu-Dej and his supporters were tolerated only as liaison men with the Rumanian masses and executors of Russian orders; their claims to leadership in the party and coformulation of policies were denied. In fact, their very political survival was assured only by the lack of suitable alternates and the temporary tying of Russia's hands by the Inter-Allied Armistice Commission established early in September. Actual power in the country rested with the Soviet High Command, and in the party, with the principal members of the Moscow Bureau, Ana Pauker and Vasile Luca.[14]

Gheorghiu-Dej and his closest associates, Chivu Stoica and Gheorghe Apostol, accepted the roles assigned to them without apparent reservations. That their differences with Moscow were not fully reconciled even after their "surrender" in August 1944 became clear only in 1952 with the purging of Ana Pauker and Vasile Luca. The failure of students of Rumanian and Communist affairs to discern the existence of an indirect struggle between Moscow and Bucharest in those years was due to their misunderstanding of Gheorghiu-Dej's tactics and positions. In the fight for political survival the Rumanian contingent concentrated on the ruthless execution of Russian-approved plans for the socialist transformation of Rumania and carefully avoided any fatal political *faux pas*. The concurrent effort to gain actual control of the party organization was carefully timed and decisive action delayed until Gheorghiu-Dej had made himself sufficiently indispensable to the Kremlin to obtain Stalin's consent to the removal of Pauker and Luca from power. In this complex process, which resulted in the

---

13 Apart from the references given in footnote 3, the reader is referred to the most illuminating statements by Gheorghiu-Dej in *Scînteia*, December 7, 1961.

14 Excellent factual information is contained in Ionescu, *Communism in Rumania*, pp. 87–99.

emergence of Gheorghiu-Dej as "boss" of Communist Rumania and of the Rumanian Communist Party, it is not always possible to distinguish between expediency and principle, between Rumanian and Russian views. However, in reviewing its principal aspects— those related to the alteration of the historic legacy through social revolution and those connected with direct or indirect Russian interference in Rumanian affairs—it is possible to discover certain consistencies in Gheorghiu-Dej's attitudes and actions which help to explain the "Rumanian course" even beyond 1952.

It is relatively easy to differentiate between the positions adopted by Gheorghiu-Dej and his associates and those of the Kremlin and its direct agents between August 1944 and the first postwar conference of the Rumanian Communist Party in October 1945. Whereas both were determined to break the power of the "historic," pro-Western political parties and to broaden the basis of popular support for the Communists, their rationale and motivations were different. In subsequent evaluations of the events of that period Gheorghiu-Dej and Ceauşescu accused Ana Pauker, and by implication the Russians, of encouraging wholesale enrollment into the party of opportunists, careerists, and fascists with subsequent alienation of "patriots" and "disillusioned progressives" from the Communist cause.[15] With allowance made for ex post facto prevarication and desire to disassociate themselves from the political actions and decisions of those days, it is incontestable that the Rumanian contingent disapproved—at least in principle—of collaboration with Iron Guardists. Opposition to fascism was particularly pronounced among the younger members who had been incarcerated during the war, whose formula for political victory stressed eradication of the "remnants of fascism" at all levels of the state apparatus and the country at large. The repeated expressions of concern over the growing power of the traditional parties, most notably the "fascist-infiltrated" National Peasant, and warnings against the dangers of indiscriminate admission of "untested" elements into the Communist Party uttered by Gheorghiu-Dej, Constantin Pârvulescu, Chivu Stoica, and others in 1944 and 1945 bear out their later contentions. That Gheorghiu-Dej and his supporters would have preferred to limit the recruitment of new party members and the assignment of responsible governmental posts to "honest" proletarians and intellectuals is also unquestionable; in

[15] See footnote 13.

practice, however, they accepted the policies dictated by General Malinovsky, the head of the Armistice Commission and of the Soviet High Command in Rumania, and executed by Ana Pauker, which were based on the need for administrative continuity and and acceptance of any converted fascist civil servant or locally influential personality into the thin ranks of the party.

It may, of course, be argued that the Russians were just as antifascist as the Rumanians and that their policies, motivated by expediency, were not irreversible. True as this may be, the Rumanians' concern with the dangers of fascism was based on more than tactical or strategic considerations. Whereas undoubtedly exaggeration of the fascist danger and accusation of the "historic" National Peasant and National Liberal parties of collusion with the enemy were designed partly to strengthen the Rumanians' argument that this national plague could be most effectively combated by Rumanians closely identified with the masses (rather than by Jews and foreigners), it is also true that Gheorghiu-Dej and his associates were more aware than Malinovsky or Pauker of the masses' political attitudes. And these attitudes were clearly unfavorable to the Communists.

It remains a matter of dispute whether the Rumanian population regarded the arrival of the Russians with any degree of enthusiasm. But whatever expectations it may have entertained in 1944 from the "liberators" were quickly dispelled by the "conquerors." Although theoretically justifiable under a broad interpretation of the provisions of the Armistice Convention, the abusive economic and political actions perpetrated by Malinovsky went beyond the rights granted the Russians in September 1944 and caused grave anxiety among the population at large. The efforts of the Rumanian leaders of the Communist Party to win the allegiance of the proletariat and peasantry met with minimal support, and the stock of the traditional parties rose rapidly. It is noteworthy, however, that the National Peasant Party, the greatest beneficiary of mass fears and suspicions, became a rallying point for anti-Communists in general rather than just the restless peasantry. It is also a fact that Maniu, the party's leader, permitted the organization to become a haven for fascists and the focus of nationalist opposition to the common Communist enemy. To a lesser degree a similar situation prevailed in the revived National Liberal Party, the stronghold of the fence-sitting Rumanian bourgeoisie and intellectuals. There can also be no doubt that both General Sănătescu and his successor General Nicolae Rădescu, as well as King Michael himself, were profoundly influenced by the leaders of these two parties and did little to disassociate themselves from fascist support. In fact, the two Sănătescu governments and that of Rădescu were distinctly anti-Russian and anti-Communist in orientation despite the fact that several members of the Communist Party, including Pătrăşcanu, Teohari Georgescu, and Gheorghiu-Dej were cabinet officers. However, unlike Ana Pauker, Vasile Luca, and their associates, who believed that the opposition could be overcome by the forcible removal of the representatives of the historic parties from these cabinets and dramatic socioeconomic action by a Communist-dominated regime, Gheorghiu-Dej and his supporters were apparently convinced that the roots of fascism—equated with bourgeois-nationalist opposition to communism—were much deeper than assumed by the Moscovites, particularly in the villages.[16] Gheorghiu-Dej and his colleagues in charge of relations with the Rumanian proletariat were also concerned about the attitudes of the workers themselves. The workers' coolness toward Communist propaganda was clearly not caused—as claimed by Gheorghiu-Dej in later years—by discouragement over the admission of fascists into the party. Rather, it was based on a fundamental distrust of the Russians fanned by the effective propaganda of the National Peasant, National Liberal, and, particularly, Social Democratic parties. The extent of fascist proclivities among the proletariat is difficult to ascertain, although it is known that Antonescu's social and economic reforms had left their imprint in the ranks of the working class. But it is a matter of record that the Social Democrats were rallying around their organization the majority of the proletariat and that the Communists were successful only in certain sectors of heavy industry and Gheorghiu-Dej's and Chivu Stoica's stronghold, the transportation industry. When, in addition, even the "progressive" urban intelligentsia—including the Jewish—was voicing suspicion of the Russians' intentions and opposition to their methods, it is clear that Gheorghiu-Dej's admonitions regarding the fascist danger and the need for a representative Communist Party were more than mere manipulations to ensure his and his associates' continuity in power.[17]

In fact, some credence may be given to later statements regarding

[16] In this connection Gheorghiu-Dej's speech of September 24, 1944 should be compared and contrasted with Pauker's of December 23, 1944. See *Scînteia*, September 25, 1944 and December 24, 1944.

[17] A careful review of the Rumanian press between August 1944 and March 1945 clarifies the political dynamics of the period as well as the functions and tactics of the Communist leaders.

the events of the crucial months immediately following the "liberation" to the effect that he and his Rumanian colleagues were fearful of civil war and that it was on their insistence that a coalition government rather than a predominantly Communist regime replaced that of General Rădescu in 1945. It is extremely doubtful—although implied by Gheorghiu-Dej in 1961—that he ever contemplated the possibility of the party's gaining power by popular consent, by securing the support of "progressive" Rumanians for a palatable social revolution. However, the evidence is conclusive in supporting his contention that, unlike Pauker and Luca, he urged caution and moderation on the Kremlin in 1944 and 1945.[18] Whether Moscow's decision to permit representation by the traditional parties in the Petru Groza government imposed upon the King by Vyshinsky in March 1945 was in any way based on Gheorghiu-Dej's recommendations is uncertain. Details on Vyshinsky's visit to Rumania in late February and early March are still vague. Nevertheless, a few indications would tend to substantiate the Rumanian contention that Gheorghiu-Dej's views were influential in the formulation of the final Russian decision.

That the Kremlin sought to remove Rădescu and the representatives of the National Liberal and National Peasant parties from the cabinet even before the Yalta Conference of February is clear. Maniu's and Dinu Brătianu's complaints of violations of the armistice provisions by Malinovsky and requests for establishment of normal diplomatic relations with the United States, Great Britain, and the Soviet Union were an anathema to Stalin. The ensuing campaign against Rădescu himself, based on his harboring fascists and thus violating the clauses of the Armistice Convention related to "democratic government," was definitely designed to allow establishment of a puppet regime without representation by the historic parties. If any excuse was needed to carry out the Russian plan, it was provided by the events of February 24, when, during a Communist-organized demonstration in Bucharest, Iron Guardist supporters of Rădescu shot into the crowd and wounded some demonstrators. Rădescu's subsequent accusation of the Communists of crimes against the Rumanian people, singling out Ana Pauker and Vasile Luca as "foreigners" and agents of Moscow, merely added fuel to the fire and triggered off Vyshinsky's mission.[19] What

18 Gheorghiu-Dej's contentions spelled out in his speech of November 30, 1961 (*Scînteia*, December 7, 1961) have been confirmed by political figures active in Rumanian affairs in 1944 and 1945.
19 *Scînteia*, February 1945, remains the primary source of information for Rumanian developments of that month.

is difficult to explain, however, is Vyshinsky's decision to settle for a compromise corresponding to Gheorghiu-Dej's formula rather than face the Western allies and Rumanian people with the *fait accompli* advocated by Pauker. One factor was undoubtedly Russia's unwillingness to play her hand too forcefully for fear of a show-down with the United States. It is still remarkable, however, that in the Groza government as it finally emerged, Communist representation was significantly smaller than that of the traditional parties. Even if Groza, the head of the Plowmen's Front, was a puppet of Moscow, the decision to maintain the façade of a broad coalition regime and to keep Ana Pauker, Vasile Luca, and all those directly identified with Moscow from ministerial posts reflects Russian awareness of the accuracy of Gheorghiu-Dej's diagnosis of the Rumanian situation. The need to identify the party's efforts with "winning the confidence of the masses" and discrediting the fascists and "allied" historic parties—whether as a direct consequence of Gheorghiu-Dej's recommendations or not—was clearly appreciated by Moscow. The formal announcement of the return of Northern Transylvania to Rumania only three days after the establishment of the Groza regime, the enactment of a sweeping land reform two weeks later, and the trial of Marshal Antonescu and his leading associates in May 1945 attest to Russia's concern.[20]

The extent of Gheorghiu-Dej's responsibility in the formulation and promotion of any of these measures remains a matter of conjecture. From the evidence available it may be surmised that his influence was secondary before the summer but that it increased sufficiently during the months of greatest crisis in postwar Rumania, August and September, to ensure acceptance by the Kremlin of his continuing tenure as Secretary-General of the Rumanian Communist Party. In the aftermath of the Potsdam Conference of July and of the related futile demand by the King, under the direct influence of Maniu, Brătianu, and other anti-Communist political leaders, for Groza's resignation, Gheorghiu-Dej sought to consolidate his position of indispensable liaison man with the Rumanian people. As the historic parties pressed their offensive against Russia— branded as an exploiter of a destitute and famished Rumania and violator of the provisions of the Armistice Convention and Potsdam Agreements—Gheorghiu-Dej outlined the Communists' long-range plans for socioeconomic reform, stressing the party's historic interest in the Rumanians' well-being as best illustrated by its organizing

---

[20] Valuable data, based on archival materials, are provided in Petric and Ţuţui, *L'instauration*, pp. 54–95.

and pursuing the country's liberation from "fascism" since August 1944. Since Ana Pauker and Vasile Luca were far too closely identified with Moscow and since, moreover, they as well as their Rumanian protégés Teohari Georgescu and Miron Constantinescu had been in no way connected with the events of August 23, 1944 and thus unable to claim credit for "liberation" of the oppressed masses, Gheorghiu-Dej could capitalize on these differences. He could also, at least *pro forma*, more readily disassociate himself from the onerous agreements setting up the infamous Soviet-Rumanian joint companies, *Sovroms* (concluded between May and August), singled out for condemnation by the opposition parties, and generally exploit the role of friend of the Rumanian people.[21] Gheorghiu-Dej's accompanying Groza to Moscow early in September as cochampion of Rumanian demands for economic assistance and easing of the terms of the Armistice Convention during the height of the famine further strengthened his position in Rumania and, *nolens volens,* also in Moscow.[22] As long as the Kremlin was as unprepared to intervene forcibly in Rumanian political affairs as it was in September 1945, Gheorghiu-Dej's survival and continuity in office were at least temporarily assured. For evidently it was in Moscow that he secured agreement to present the political report to the Conference of the Rumanian Communist Party and be elected Secretary-General one month later.

The Rumanian Communists now claim to be the executors of the program submitted by Gheorghiu-Dej at the conference and trace their conflict with Russia to Moscow's and her representatives' interference with the implementation of that program's provisions. Under the circumstances it may well be asked whether Gheorghiu-Dej's plans for the country's socialist transformation were incompatible with Russian interests. The most careful analysis of the proceedings of the conference and related documents reveals no overt incompatibilities whatever.[23] However, it is clear that the prevailing mutual suspicions were not buried with the adoption of the program and election of Gheorghiu-Dej in October 1945. Gheorghiu-Dej must have realized the long-range implications of Soviet economic penetration through the *Sovroms,* but it is far from certain

---

21 Compare speeches by Gheorghiu-Dej, Ana Pauker, and Vasile Luca made on the occasion of the anniversary of Rumania's "liberation from fascism" in *Scînteia,* August 23, 1945.

22 *Ibid.,* September 14, 1945.

23 The materials relevant to the October Conference will be found in *ibid.,* October 18–22, 1945. For Gheorghiu-Dej's political report, see *ibid.,* October 20, 1945.

that he was even secretly opposed to the establishment of the joint stock companies in 1945. His own and his supporters' primary interests—at that time, political survival and socioeconomic change —could not be attained by alternate means. It is possible, even probable, that, like Pătrăşcanu, Gheorghiu-Dej would have preferred to bring about the socialist transformation of Rumania without exclusive dependence on Russia. However, unlike Pătrăşcanu, he was totally unwilling to risk his political future on principles. To strengthen his own position, he was fully prepared to disassociate himself from Pătrăşcanu altogether and to press for his removal from the Politburo at the October Conference. On the other hand, Gheorghiu-Dej himself was by no means above suspicion, and it is evident that he was still only tolerated by Moscow and his "superiors" in the party in the fall of 1945. The tactical strength derived from his group's identification with the masses and contribution to the country's "liberation" was clearly a point of friction, as evidenced by the constant omission of any reference to the Rumanians' contribution to that liberation by the "Moscovites" and their attempts to seek closer ties with the Rumanian people through other native Rumanians not connected with the Gheorghiu-Dej group. The search for and creation of Rumanian alternates, started in September 1944, was theoretically sufficiently advanced by October 1945 to allow at least the packing of the Central Committee, Politburo, and Secretariat with Moscovites and their Rumanian protégés. In the all-important Secretariat of the Central Committee, for instance, Gheorghiu-Dej was surrounded by Pauker, Luca, and Georgescu, while in the Politburo Pauker and Luca's Rumanians, Georgescu and Constantinescu, could readily outvote Gheorghiu-Dej and Stoica in the company of their protectors.[24] Nevertheless, despite his position of relative weakness, Gheorghiu-Dej had scored a crucial victory. Having secured the post that he was to retain until death, he altered his tactics sufficiently to consolidate his gains.

The essential difference between Gheorghiu-Dej's actions during the years before and immediately after the conference was his assumption of the role of liaison man with Moscow in matters related

[24] The actual composition of the "Moscovite" and "Rumanian" groups is not easy to ascertain. It is clear, however, that Miron Constantinescu, Teohari Georgescu, and Iosif Chişinevski were identified with the Pauker-Luca axis while Apostol, Ceauşescu, and Chivu Stoica were loyal to Gheorghiu-Dej. Bodnăraş's position was apparently one of neutrality; he may very well have been the "swing man" even at that early date.

to implementing the economic goals of the party's program. Taking advantage of the Kremlin's endorsement of the plans for Rumania's "socialist transformation" as presented at the conference, Gheorghiu-Dej succeeded in interposing himself sufficiently between the Moscovites and the Kremlin by 1947 to emerge as a trustworthy servant of Stalin. At the same time he was able to preserve the strategic advantage derived from direct identification with the Rumanian plan for socioeconomic revolution and the corollary incorporation into the party apparatus of supporters directly concerned with the country's industrialization.

The years 1946 and 1947 provided the necessary opportunities for implementation of this strategy, at least to the extent of ensuring his survival as Secretary-General even after the need for "gaining the confidence of the people" and of maintaining the façade of coalition government as much as disappeared by late 1947. Since Russia agreed in December 1945, at least *pro forma,* to American and British demands for the "broadening of the basis" of the Groza regime preliminary to the holding of free elections and conclusion of the peace treaty with Rumania, Gheorghiu-Dej assumed the position of the party's campaign manager for the Groza government, exhorting the patriotic sentiments of the population. Whether invoking the party's historic interest in the people's well-being, advancing the claims of Communist succession to the revolutionary legacy of 1848, or, most blatantly, appealing directly to the "Rumanian" sentiments of the electorate, Gheorghiu-Dej and his closest associates constantly reiterated their contribution to their country's "liberation." However, Gheorghiu-Dej gradually introduced the notions of the indispensability of Russian assistance for the execution of the party's program and of Russia's "eternal friendship" as proved by Moscow's own share in the freeing of the Rumanians from fascism and generosity in times of need.[25] In this manner it was at least theoretically easy for him to justify by mid-1946 the abandonment of the oft-mentioned concept of "cobelligerency" and its replacement by that of "fraternal friendship."

It is now evident that one of Gheorghiu-Dej's most masterful moves was made during the negotiations for the Rumanian peace treaty in the summer of 1946. As the only Communist member of the Rumanian delegation besides Pătrăşcanu, he became the principal spokesman for Stalin's views. The Russians were adamantly opposed to granting the status of "cobelligerent" to the Rumanians

25 See major pronunciamentos in *Scînteia,* March 7, May 18, and July 8, 1946.

since such recognition would have weakened the legal and pragmatic basis for military, political, and economic action in Rumania. To strengthen the appearance of friendship for the Rumanian people and of concern for the country's well-being, they agreed, however, formally to reduce the economic claims awarded them by the Armistice Convention. If Gheorghiu-Dej was not a party to Russian decisions, he was ready to carry out Moscow's orders during the protracted negotiations, realizing at all times that the so-called concessions made by the Kremlin merely provided the means for unilateral milking of the Rumanian economy and for unequivocal establishment of Russian control over Rumania. Nevertheless, as a political realist Gheorghiu-Dej took full advantage of the role assigned to him by Moscow. In October, as Stalin's aims became increasingly more evident even in Rumania, Gheorghiu-Dej returned from Paris to participate in the electoral campaign, pressing the theme of the party's identification with the Rumanian masses and of Moscow's friendship and generosity toward Rumania.[26] Whether as a reflection of the control exerted at the polls or of actual popularity with the electorate in his own (railwaymen's) district, Gheorghiu-Dej rolled up the largest plurality of all candidates submitted by the Communist-controlled People's Democratic Front in Bucharest in the rigged elections of November 19. It is noteworthy, however, that he did not return to Paris to sign the peace treaty in February 1947.

It is doubtful that his absence could be attributed to foresight, to conscious disassociation from a document politically unpopular and detrimental to the execution of Rumanian plans for economic development. The evidence does not corroborate later intimations and allegations to that effect any more than similar ones concerning Gheorghiu-Dej's alleged favoring of Rumanian participation in the Marshall Plan.[27] On the contrary, his absence can be best accounted for by his awareness that Russia would not relinquish any of its gains and that his own future was inexorably connected with subservience to the Kremlin. The acceptance of a full-fledged satellite status for himself and Rumania may also have been motivated by genuine interest in the realization of the party's long-range goals for economic development. This thesis, propounded by the Ruma-

[26] *Scînteia,* October 28, 1946, contains several articles of major relevance in this connection.

[27] Exploratory conversations between Burton Berry and Gheorghiu-Dej were apparently held as early as May 1947. Gheorghiu-Dej evinced only the most rudimentary interest in any program of economic recovery from the very beginning and refused to participate after consultation with Moscow.

nians, is essentially tenable, but concern for strengthening his own position was paramount at least in 1947. Gheorghiu-Dej's presence in Moscow, during the month of the signing of the peace treaty, for negotiation of another onerous Russo-Rumanian economic agreement—publicized, however, as another expression of Russian concern for Rumania's well-being—would be difficult to explain in terms of Rumania's long-range interests alone. On the other hand, the promises of economic reform and stabilization of the currency made by Gheorghiu-Dej on June 14 only a few days after the formulation of the Marshall Plan may be explained both by his desire as the minister in charge of economic affairs and Secretary-General of the party to remove all doubts of loyalty to Stalin and by the realities of internal political and economic conditions.[28] After a hurried visit to Moscow he knew that the Russians would reject the American plan and that the end of the coalition government, the removal of the last representatives of the historic parties, and their replacement by reliable Moscovites were imminent. The prospective "unleashing" of Ana Pauker and Vasile Luca must have been disconcerting. For despite his efforts as Secretary-General to alter the balance of power in the party, Pauker, Luca, and their close associates had maintained their firm grip on the Central Committee, Politburo, and Secretariat and packed the ranks of the organization with elements subservient to themselves. Although the enrollment of members of the Rumanian working class and "honest intellectuals"—advocated by Gheorghiu-Dej and his supporters— was gaining momentum, the Moscovites' recruitment of veterans of the Russian-trained Tudor Vladimirescu brigade of Rumanian "volunteers" who fought alongside the Russian "liberators" during the war more than offset the gains recorded by the "Rumanians." Because of this imbalance, Gheorghiu-Dej apparently decided to consolidate his own position with Moscow without, however, abandoning his traditional role of leader of the "liberation" of the masses and exponent of their "true" interests. In assuming the direction of the economic stabilization program in August 1947, Gheorghiu-Dej became at the same time the executor of the Kremlin's wishes and of the party's program for economic development for the benefit of the Rumanian people. Thus, when Ana Pauker became Minister of Foreign Affairs and Vasile Luca Minister of Finance in November, at the time of the formal destruction of the historic parties through the removal of the last Liberals from the

28 *Scînteia,* June 14 and 16, 1947.

Groza cabinet and the conviction of Maniu and other National Peasant leaders "for political crimes against the Rumanian people," Gheorghiu-Dej was formally concentrating on the development of a "socialist" economy in Rumania. He was also in that position when the monarchy was abolished and the Rumanian People's Democracy proclaimed on December 30, 1947.[29]

With the abandonment of all pretense to socioeconomic change within the political framework inherited by the Communists at the end of the war and imposed upon them and Moscow by the United States and Great Britain, the problems confronting the party and government assumed a markedly different character. The process of "socialist transformation" was formally entrusted to the Communist Party, and the struggle for power and survival centered entirely on inter- and intraparty relationships. Ultimately, all decisions were to be made or approved by Moscow. Seeking the support of the masses became an entirely secondary concern to the Communists as the notion of class struggle replaced that of "winning the confidence of the people." In this new framework of action Gheorghiu-Dej's weapons were blunted but not totally discarded. They stood him in good stead in times of crisis and eventually proved decisive in the attainment of his primary goal—assumption of complete control over the party apparatus. While his tactics and maneuvers in the crucial years 1948–1952 were tortuous, they were at all times characterized by prudence and subservience toward Moscow. And although apparently unscrupulous they could be justified as essential for the attainment of the party's program and the corollary ultimate happiness of the Rumanian people.

The first opportunity to consolidate his gains under the dual formula of total subservience to the Kremlin and director of the socialist destiny of the Rumanians occurred in February 1948, at the First Congress of the newly established Rumanian Workers' Party. The fusion of the Rumanian Communist Party with the left-wing contingent of the dismembered Social Democratic Party— desired by Moscow for tactical purposes in the fall of 1947—was effectuated at the Union Congress of February 21–23.[30] The influx by new Rumanian workers, former members of the Social Democratic Party, into the new Rumanian Workers' Party altered the

[29] Important information on these points may be found in Ionescu, *Communism in Rumania*, pp. 126–143, 204–208.

[30] The proceedings of the congress may be found in *Scînteia*, February 22–24, 1948.

social composition of the organization to benefit Gheorghiu-Dej. At least as beneficial was the reduction of the proportion of Moscovites in the Central Committee through the inclusion of the elite of the Social Democratic leadership. The ensuing Rumanianization of the Central Committee meant relatively little per se given the unchanged balance of forces in the Secretariat. It did, however, provide Gheorghiu-Dej with a larger number of supporters theoretically identified with the Rumanian working class. And the fusion itself allowed him subsequently to undertake, on his initiative as Secretary-General of the new party, the revision of the credentials of all members. The Union Congress also permitted Gheorghiu-Dej to restate in more specific terms the Communist goals for the country's economic development, the party's historic interest in the people's happiness, its eternal gratitude to the Soviet Union, and to deliver an unequivocal condemnation of the principal political crimes committed by the defunct traditional parties and former members of the Groza government—chauvinism, bourgeois nationalism, and economic sabotage.[31] It is, however, significant that it was Teohari Georgescu rather than Gheorghiu-Dej who levied similar accusations against Lucreţiu Pătrăşcanu in reading him out of the Central Committee.

The specific charges against Pătrăşcanu, spelled out in greater detail in June when Moscow's break with Tito became official, were primarily designed to exonerate the leadership of any possible suspicion of Titoism by singling out the party's former leader as a supporter of Yugoslav heresies. Nevertheless, in view of Luca's subsequent intimations of Gheorghiu-Dej's endorsement of Pătrăşcanu's policies in 1944[32] and Gheorghiu's own "Titoism" of later years, it has been suggested that Georgescu's speech of February 22 was also intended to cast doubts on the orthodoxy of the Secretary-General. There can be no question about Pătrăşcanu's Titoist proclivities and constant advocacy of a course that would prevent Rumania's reduction to a vassal state of the Soviet Union. However, Gheorghiu-Dej's disassociation from Pătrăşcanu was complete by 1946; and even if he secretly entertained sentiments comparable to Pătrăşcanu's and Tito's, such were hardly in evidence. Gheorghiu-Dej personally denounced Pătrăşcanu's "chauvinist" and "revisionist" tendencies in July 1946,[33] to prove his faithfulness to Moscow. If anything, he was more careful than Ana Pauker on the occasion

---

31 See Gheorghiu-Dej's political report in *ibid.*, February 22, 1948.
32 See page 40.
33 *Scînteia*, July 8, 1946.

of Tito's state visit to Rumania in December 1947.[34] Gheorghiu-Dej was also extremely alert to Moscow's displeasure with any form of independent Communist action on the occasion of Georgi Dimitrov's visit to Bucharest in January 1948, when, like Ana Pauker, he carefully refrained from endorsing the Bulgarian leader's plans for a Communist Balkan federation.[35] And during the ensuing pilgrimage to Moscow, in the company of Groza, Luca, and Pauker, which resulted in the long-term treaty of "friendship, collaboration, and mutual assistance" with the Soviet Union, he clearly received the Kremlin's absolution and blessings for continuation in office as Secretary-General. However, even if Gheorghiu-Dej was given a clean bill of health by Stalin in February, it would appear that the Moscovites sought to consolidate their own position in the Romanized and enlarged Rumanian Workers' Party by utilizing a weapon exclusively their own—nonparticipation in Rumanian affairs prior to Russia's "liberation" of the country in 1944. Evidently, in the atmosphere of mutual suspicion, domestic and international, that prevailed in the weeks preceding Yugoslavia's formal expulsion from the Cominform, total, traditional, and preferably exclusive identification with Moscow was fortifying, perhaps invaluable, à tout.

Though the evidence regarding the Moscovites' intentions in February 1948 is somewhat inconclusive, it is clear that Gheorghiu-Dej promptly undertook a series of decisive moves to counteract any possible suspicions of his loyalty to Moscow and at least one major action directed expressly against Ana Pauker and her associates. On June 10 he announced that on his own request the Soviet Union had agreed to reduce the reparation payments by 50 per cent;[36] on June 11 he warned all "class enemies" guilty of "chauvinism" and "bourgeois" nationalism, including those in the party, of their forthcoming doom;[37] and on July 1, immediately after Tito's formal excommunication, he published a most virulent denunciation of the Yugoslavs' heresies and hostility toward the Soviet Union and the Soviet Communist Party.[38] These moves were carefully calculated and had far-reaching implications. The announcement of the reduction of Soviet reparation payments, coinciding with the nationalization of industry, gave support to his contention that Rumania's

[34] *Ibid.*, December 18–24, 1947.
[35] *Ibid.*, January 15–19, 1948.
[36] *Ibid.*, June 10, 1948.
[37] *Ibid.*, June 22, 1948.
[38] *Ibid.*, July 3, 1948.

economic development, as programmed and directed by him, met with the total approval of the Soviet Union. In assuming the role of champion of Stalinist doctrinal purity, he placed himself in the position of grand inquisitor wherefrom he could weaken and discredit his opponents. The means chosen, revision of the party's membership to root out the class enemy—the fascists and careerists enrolled by Pauker and Constantinescu in 1944 and 1945—was a direct challenge to the Moscovites which they could not prevent in the wake of their own denunciation of Pătrășcanu and Stalin's of Tito. In fact, the formal approval by the Central Committee of the Secretary-General's request for revision in November marked the beginning of the direct conflict between Gheorghiu-Dej and Pauker.[39] By placing himself in the forefront of the socioeconomic and political revolution under these circumstances, Gheorghiu-Dej incurred at least two major risks: total alienation of the Rumanian masses and Stalin's wrath. In overcoming the first and preventing the second lies the secret of his victory in 1952.

The fundamental problem facing Gheorghiu-Dej in 1948 and the years immediately following was the destruction of all obstacles to the attainment of the Stalinist prescription of rapid industrialization, agricultural collectivization, and delivery of products to the Soviet Union on the basis of existing treaty obligations eminently unfavorable to the Rumanians. There is no evidence, his own statements notwithstanding, that in the execution of these requirements he assumed positions essentially different from those of his rivals for power in the party. The basic economic measures adopted before September 1951—the beginning of economic planning in 1948 and of agricultural collectivization in 1949 as well as all other lesser measures connected with economic development—were evidently approved by the highest party echelons without dissent. Nor is it possible, before 1951, to differentiate between the basic views on the pursuit of the class struggle of Gheorghiu-Dej, Ana Pauker, and Vasile Luca. The ferocity of the assault on the bourgeoisie, former landowning class, kulaks, intellectual community in general, religious organizations, foreign nationals, and all others suspect of "fascist" and "antidemocratic" tendencies was repeatedly justified by Gheorghiu-Dej even more vociferously than by the others.[40] Tac-

---

39 A detailed account of the process of revision and its results is given by Gheorghiu-Dej in the article "Für die Reinheit der Partei," *Für dauerhaften Frieden, für Volksdemokratie!*, June 23, 1950.

40 See, for instance, his article "Der Klassenkampf in Rumänien in der gegenwärtigen Etappe," *ibid.*, April 7, 1950.

tically, his total commitment to the Stalinist prescription had certain advantages. It could be justified, as it was, in terms of the Rumanian people's own good and his unsurpassed awareness of the real obstacles to the attainment of the party's historic goals. By 1950 the repeated advocacy of the concept that it took a Rumanian to know a Rumanian was beginning to pay off and cause a major counteroffensive by the non-Rumanians in the party, Ana Pauker and Vasile Luca.

The evidence as provided both by Gheorghiu-Dej's and Ceauşescu's indictments of the "antiparty" group in 1961 and by earlier statements and documents bearing on the removal of Pauker, Luca, and Georgescu in 1952 pinpoints the spring of 1950 as the period of the first major confrontation between Gheorghiu-Dej and his opponents.[41] No matter what the official reasons for Pauker's, Luca's, and Georgescu's removal from power in 1952, the real ones are solely connected with the struggle for control of the party. Gheorghiu-Dej was moving rapidly toward victory by the spring of 1950, when the results of the revision of the party's membership were made public. The length of the verification process attests not so much to its thoroughness as to the importance attached to its outcome by the pro- and anti-Gheorghiu-Dej forces. Gheorghiu-Dej's men—Ranghet, Moghioroş and Pârvulescu—were technically in charge of the investigations and accompanying purges that resulted in the removal of 192,000 "fascists," "careerists," and "opportunists" by June 1950. Because the regular recruitment since 1948 was limited primarily to industrial workers and alumni of the Union of Working Youth (*Uniunea Tineretului Muncitoresc—UTM*), dominated by Nicolae Ceauşescu, the party after verification consisted largely of elements identified with Gheorghiu-Dej's "Rumanians." Gheorghiu-Dej promptly exploited that victory. On June 23, 1950, in the Cominform journal, he denounced the errors in recruitment by those in charge of that process in the immediate postwar period and pledged the replacement of "hostile elements" still ensconced in the party organization by men and women of "healthy social origin."[42] The thinly disguised conclusion that the Rumanian Workers' Party must be the party of Rumanian workers was unmistakably clear to

---

41 *Scînteia*, December 7, 1961. Also *Documents Concerning Right Wing Deviation in Rumanian Workers' Party* (Bucharest: Rumanian Workers' Party Publishing House, 1952), pp. 3–85 (hereafter cited as *Documents*); and *Rezoluţii şi hotărîri ale Comitetului Central al Partidului Muncitoresc Român* [Resolutions and Decisions of the Central Committee of the Rumanian Workers' Party] (Bucharest: Editura pentru Literatura Politică, 1954), Vol. II (1951–1953), pp. 5–189, hereafter cited as *Rezoluţii*.
42 See footnote 39.

Pauker and Luca, who sought to counteract Gheorghiu's advantage by strengthening their grip on the Secretariat and by seeking to discredit him with the Rumanian masses and with the Kremlin. Between the summer of 1950 and the spring of 1952 the Moscovites tried to pin the blame for Rumania's difficulties on the unreliable Gheorghiu-Dej and his associates. In turn, Gheorghiu-Dej sought to maintain his tactical advantage by levying similar charges against his opponents.

Ana Pauker, Vasile Luca, and Teohari Georgescu sought first to appease the dissatisfied peasantry. The attitude of the peasant masses became a matter of concern to the party in 1950, particularly after the outbreak of the Korean War. As fears of a possible showdown with the Western "imperialists" increased in Stalin's empire, enlarged agricultural and industrial productivity (and deliveries to Russia) and avoidance of peasant unrest were imperative. Pauker had been in charge of the implementation of agricultural collectivization from as early as 1949. By mid-1950 she apparently began to deviate from the prescribed line in order to disassociate herself from policies that met with massive resistance in the villages. The decision to slow down the collectivization drive early in 1951 and to encourage kulak production was, it would seem, made by the Moscovites, independently of Gheorghiu-Dej's preference for continued socialization of agriculture.[43] This "right-wing deviation" contributed to their eventual downfall, as Gheorghiu-Dej was able by September 1951 to nullify their advantage. Invoking the mandate for postverification reform, after the elections of March 1951, he packed the regional and local party organizations with elements "close to the masses," thus assuming virtual control over the entire apparatus short of the Secretariat.[44] Pauker's and Luca's most significant retaliatory effort was made on August 23, when in an unprecedented move Luca gave the principal address on the occasion of the seventh anniversary of Rumania's liberation. He pointed an accusing finger at Gheorghiu-Dej and his associates by recalling the errors of 1944 and unequivocally crediting the "glorious Soviet armies" for the country's liberation. The contemporary shortcomings in agriculture and deficiencies in the rate of industrial production were also less than discreetly attributed to the "Rumanians."[45] Luca, however, miscalculated both Moscow's responsiveness to these charges and Gheorghiu-Dej's own retaliatory powers.

43 See footnote 41.
44 *Rezoluţii*, pp. 36–55.
45 *Scînteia*, August 23, 1951.

In September, posing as the proved friend of the peasantry, the latter was able to obtain a party resolution criticizing arbitrary departures from the guidelines of agricultural collectivization set in 1949 and urging the establishment of voluntary agricutural associations (of the Soviet TOZ-type) that safeguarded the peasant's property and profit rights.[46] Also to demonstrate his doctrinal purity he proposed another currency reform designed to wipe out kulaks and urban speculators.[47] It is believed that Luca opposed the latter measure, favoring alleviation rather than exacerbation of economic pressures and of the class struggle in town and village. In this he was apparently supported by Ana Pauker, since both sought to gain Moscow's endorsement for that course.[48] Gheorghiu-Dej, exploiting his own strength in the party, reinforced his own claims to the role of champion of Rumanian interests and defender of Stalinist orthodoxy early in November when a "spontaneous" celebration was staged by the organization in honor of his fiftieth birthday. Nationwide eulogies for his contribution to the party and the Rumanian people were designed to mark him as the indispensable man for the attainment of Russian and Rumanian goals. However, his position was apparently not as secure with the Kremlin as with his followers in Rumania because he found it necessary to take a public oath of loyalty to Stalin when he assured ". . . the Central Committee of the Communist (Bolshevik) Party of the Soviet Union and Comrade Stalin personally that he will be a faithful soldier of the cause of Lenin and Stalin."[49] Since Ana Pauker had only two days earlier publicly stressed her own unmistakable loyalty to Stalin, it would appear that the doors to the Kremlin were still open to the opposing factions at that time.[50] Pauker's access must have become more limited, and Luca's ended altogether in the following few weeks as the course proposed by Gheorghiu-Dej was implemented in January 28, 1952 with the announcement of the drastic currency reform. By the end of February Gheorghiu-Dej must have considered himself in a sufficiently strong position to accuse Luca, Pauker, and Georgescu of "deviationism" at the Plenum of the Central Committee.[51] And, presumably, he took no major risks when at a second plenum held late in May he succeeded in having Luca and Georgescu removed from their party posts and

46 *Rezoluții*, pp. 67–110.
47 *Ibid.*, pp. 130–150.
48 *Documents*, pp. 5–28 and 33–62.
49 *Scînteia*, November 9, 1951.
50 *Ibid.*, November 7, 1951.
51 *Ibid.*, March 7, 1952; *Documents*, pp. 5–28.

Ana Pauker from the Politburo and Secretariat.[52] On May 29 Gheorghiu-Dej emerged as the *de facto* leader of the Rumanian Workers' Party, and on June 2 he also assumed the premiership of the Rumanian government. On June 3, in his acceptance speech to the Grand National Assembly, he pledged economic reform, correction of the abuses perpetrated by Luca and Georgescu and condoned by Pauker, and further strengthening of ties with the Soviet Union.[53]

The significance of the events of the spring of 1952 remains difficult to ascertain. The fundamental question of whether they were anti-Russian in nature or motivated by a genuine interest in establishing a Rumanian basis for the building of socialism in Rumania cannot be answered in unequivocal terms. All factors considered, it is probable that Gheorghiu-Dej assumed certain risks in purging Luca and Georgescu and demoting Ana Pauker, but he did not face the Kremlin with a *fait accompli*. It is improbable that the Plenum's decision of May 26–27 was taken totally independently of Moscow, and the very retention of Pauker in the Central Committee and Orgburo tends to indicate that the Kremlin's permission for reorganization was far from comprehensive. Whether the replacement in the Secretariat of Luca and Georgescu by Chişinevski and Constantinescu was the price of the Kremlin's consent for the Moscovites' removal or whether Gheorghiu-Dej himself found it necessary to limit the spring cleaning for fear of Russian retaliation remains a matter of speculation.[54] Most probably he acted on the assumption that internal change involving the substitution of Stalinists for Moscovites, in the name of greater efficiency, was a safe course. Stalin's pronunciamentos on "cosmopolitanism" and related purges in the bloc and the constant Russian demands for strengthening the economies of the satellites provided him with such margin of safety as may have been necessary.[55] In any case, it is clear that the "Rumanians" did not score a complete victory in 1952 if the motive

52 *Rezoluţii*, pp. 188–189.

53 *Scînteia*, June 3–4, 1952.

54 Constantinescu's position in June 1952 was somewhat different from Chişinevski's. Although an orthodox Communist he leaned to the "right," favoring relaxation of pressures on the masses to ensure a more effective common effort in the "building of socialism." Chişinevski's views were closer to Gheorghiu-Dej's, favoring rigorous execution of existing plans.

55 Gheorghiu-Dej did not accuse his opponents of "cosmopolitanism" directly. However, Ana Pauker's Jewish background and entourage made her vulnerable to such charges and facilitated her removal from power in a country with a pronounced tradition of anti-Semitism.

for their actions transcended that of removing Moscow's direct agents from the Secretariat. On the other hand, following the reorganization of the Politburo and Secretariat, the possibility of radical Russian intervention in the party's internal affairs was markedly reduced. Even if the Rumanians held only a slim majority in the new Secretariat and Politburo, it was still sufficient to alter the balance of power in their favor.[56]

The related question of whether Gheorghiu-Dej's continuing subservience to the Soviet Union, with resultant retardation of such plans for the improvement of Rumanian economic conditions as he may have had, was due entirely to the prevailing power relationship between Moscow and Bucharest or whether his goal in the spring of 1952 was essentially that of consolidating his own power in the refurbished establishment also defies a categorical answer. Nothing in the evidence could substantiate the view that he was concerned at the time with the well-being of the Rumanian people per se or that he contemplated any appropriate changes in internal or foreign policy.[57] However, such evidence would be inconclusive in disproving his actually not having reformist intentions under the "objective conditions" of 1952. In any event, in June 1952 Gheorghiu-Dej assumed control of the party and government as the exponent of doctrinaire Stalinism and of rigid measures for the total extirpation of those aspects of the historic legacy—most notably peasant opposition to communism and "bourgeois nationalism" with its corollary anti-Russianism—which could have in any way jeopardized his relationships with the Kremlin and the execution of existing plans for Rumania's socialist transformation as a faithful Soviet satellite.

[56] Of the nine members of the Politburo Gheorgiu-Dej apparently could count on the support of Moghioroș, Apostol, Stoica, and Pârvulescu on most major issues. In the Secretariat Moghioroș and Apostol counterbalanced, at least numerically, Chişinevski and Constantinescu. The composition of the Politburo and the Secretariat may be found in *Documents*, pp. 31–32.

[57] *Scînteia*, June 3–4, 1952; *Documents*, pp. 63–85.

CHAPTER THREE

"RECULER POUR MIEUX SAUTER" (*1952–1960*)

Any search for clues to the origins of Rumanian policies in any way independent of the Kremlin would be frustrating if based on an analysis of events antedating Stalin's death. It would, however, be fruitful in seeking out the reasons for the adoption of the "New Course"—the forerunner of the "independent course" of later years—in August 1953.

The striking feature of Rumanian politics following Gheorghiu-Dej's victory was his championing of the most rigid Stalinist positions in internal affairs and his constant denunciation of the "anti-party" group for right-wing deviationism and appeasement. The need to be more Stalinist than Stalin seemingly reflected uncertainty over a delayed reaction by Ana Pauker's supporters in the Kremlin—later identified as Malenkov and Beria—and by the Rumanian party itself more than fear of internal unrest by the dissatisfied masses. The constant invocation of Stalin's dicta on revolutionary vigilance, doctrinal purity, and related topics was clearly designed to check the spread of "heresies" among the apparently responsive rank and file of the party and to prevent the rise of a middle-of-the-road Stalinist, such as Miron Constantinescu, in a manner that could upset the balance of power in the organization.[1] Constantinescu actually did represent a potential threat to Gheorghiu-Dej both as a friend of Moscow and as a patron of a still-substantial segment of the party's membership. Constantinescu's own positions in those months are difficult to ascertain. However, if one considers the events immediately preceding and following Stalin's death, certain differences between Constantinescu's and Gheorghiu-Dej's views become apparent. It was Gheorghiu-Dej

[1] See, for instance, Gheorghiu-Dej's speech on the occasion of the anniversary of Rumania's liberation, *Scînteia*, August 23, 1952, and his report to the Grand National Assembly on the Draft of the Constitution of the Rumanian People's Republic, *ibid.*, September 24, 1952. The most eloquent tribute to Stalin is contained in his article "Stalin, eliberatorul popoarelor" [Stalin, the Peoples' Liberator], *ibid.*, March 8, 1953.

44

who equated the party's historic plans and principles for the socialist transformation of Rumania with those of Stalin, thus preempting the role of Stalin's deputy and champion of Rumanian interests. Constantinescu, as a nonparticipant in the formulation of the historic goals of the party, sought identification with current socialist construction as Rumania's chief economic planner. As such he signed the principal economic agreement with the Soviet Union establishing two new *Sovroms* in August 1952, and he repeatedly advocated the strengthening of ties with the Soviet Union. It is very doubtful that Gheorghiu-Dej allowed him to assume the role of direct intermediary between the Rumanian party and the Kremlin in economic affairs on the belief that Constantinescu would dig his own grave in the event of continuing economic difficulties. In fact, both Gheorghiu-Dej and Constantinescu were convinced that economic conditions, precarious as they were in the summer of 1952, would improve sooner or later through cooperation with Moscow and that such results would strengthen Constantinescu's position in Rumania. That all was not well in those days between the two men became public knowledge in 1957 after the purge of Constantinescu and Iosif Chişinevski from the Rumanian Workers' Party.[2]

Gheorghiu-Dej's continuing servitude to Stalin and advocacy of the modified historic line allowed him, *inter alia,* to pursue the "struggle against the class enemy" in the party and to eliminate a potential base of support for Constantinescu and any other possible rival. His overriding concern with consolidation of his hold on the party is manifest in the several decisions of the Central Committee and public statements devoted to revision, purity, and rooting out of supporters of Luca, Pauker, and Georgescu. These matters had priority over winning mass support for his line even at a time when he deemed it essential to legitimize his political actions through the issuance of a new constitution. In none of the speeches made during the campaign for public acceptance of the new fundamental law did Gheorghiu-Dej hold out the prospect of rapid im-

2 Gheorghiu-Dej's version of Constantinescu's plans and activities was first spelled out in July 1957 following Constantinescu's removal from power (*Scînteia,* July 9, 1957). A more detailed indictment of the deposed leader was provided by Gheorghiu-Dej in December 1961 in his report to the Plenum of the party's Central Committee relative to the proceedings of the CPSU Twenty-Second Congress (*ibid.,* December 7, 1961). Constantinescu's prominence in the immediate post-Pauker period is revealed by the number of significant speeches delivered on major topics on special occasions. Typical of his views are those contained in the interminable address on the occasion of the thirty-fifth anniversary of the October Revolution printed in full in *ibid.,* November 7, 1952.

provement of the country's economy, departure from rigorous enforcement of existing plans and policies, or tolerance toward the omnipresent class enemy.[3] The constitution itself was a rigidly orthodox document granting unlimited powers to the party and providing the authority—if such were needed—for ruthless pursuit of the process of socialist construction à la Stalin and Gheorghiu-Dej. At the time of Stalin's death Gheorghiu-Dej's commitment to Stalinism at home and Russia abroad was complete. But was it profound?

In 1953 the answer to this fundamental question would have been unequivocally yes. Gheorghiu-Dej was a disciple of Stalin and a devoted servant of Moscow by conviction as well as by necessity. Nowhere in his contemporary speeches or actions, or even subsequent recollections and reinterpretation of the events of the early fifties, is it possible to find any indication of disassociation from Stalin and Russia. Gheorghiu-Dej was convinced that his maintenance in power and execution of the plans for the socialist transformation of Rumania required strong-arm methods. He was keenly aware of the profound dissatisfaction of the masses with his policies, of the popular hatred of Russia, communism, and the Rumanian Workers' Party. And whereas he did not expect the class enemy to be able to stage a successful counterrevolution owing to the reign of police terror and the reliability of the Russian troops stationed in the country, he was conscious of the fact that the unreliability of the masses was a deterrent to the execution of the obligations imposed upon Rumania by Stalin and himself. These problems were to be overcome by relentless assaults on production goals and the "enemies of the new order" and only when absolutely necessary by token concessions. In the party too he was identified with Stalinist rigidity and maintained his power through reliance on hand-picked "leading cadres."[4] It is a matter of speculation as to what Gheorghiu-Dej's future would have been had Stalin lived only a few months longer than he did or had he veered in the direction of accommodation with the West. In death, however, the Russian dictator left Gheorghiu-Dej in the critical position of a dyed-in-the-wool Stalinist at a time of transition in Soviet policy from war—both hot and cold—to peaceful coexistence, do-

---

3 *Rezoluții și hotărîri ale comitetului central al Partidului Muncitoresc Român* (Bucharest: Editura pentru Literatura Politică, 1954), Vol. II (1951–1953), pp. 209–315 (hereafter cited as *Rezoluții*). See Gheorghiu-Dej's key electoral speech in *Scînteia*, November 29, 1952.

4 The texts of the principal decisions and resolutions of the Rumanian party speak for themselves. *Rezoluții*, Vol. II, pp. 316–540.

mestic and foreign. Gheorghiu's maneuvers, worthy of his political skills, hold the key to any meaningful explanation of the "New Course" of 1953 and of the "independent course" of later years.

Stalin's death, the subsequent relaxation of pressures in the Soviet Union, the search for improved relations with the West, and, above all, the struggle for power in the Kremlin forced Gheorghiu-Dej to protect his interests on a multilateral basis. The course chosen in the early months of the Malenkov era was one of seeking consolidation of his own power in the party in his role of traditional guardian of Rumanian interests and champion of the historical goals of the Rumanian people, greater identification of the party and its programs with the masses, and development of a clearer Rumanian national identity in foreign affairs. His motivations were political even if the principal manifestation of the strategic measures adopted after March 1953 was the "New Course" for economic development. For no matter how the change of leadership would affect Russian domestic and foreign policies, Gheorghiu-Dej's own position vis-à-vis Moscow and in Rumania itself could only be strengthened through improvement of domestic economic conditions.[5] It is probable that the extensive program of economic reform decided on by the plenum of the party's Central Committee on August 19–20, 1953 reflected the composite view of the entire leadership. The less heralded but ultimately more important "Decision on the Improvement of Party Work and Relations of the Party with the Masses," adopted at the same time, revealed serious internal problems.[6] The Decision was a frontal attack against the irregularities and unhealthy practices condoned and promoted by Luca, Pauker, and Georgescu (and, by implication, by Pauker's assistant recruiter, Constantinescu) and a mandate to Gheorghiu-Dej's men to do away not only with these nefarious practices but also with those party members inclined to believe that Stalin's death would result in abandonment of Stalinist principles and practices. The call for continuous vigilance and purges was far more strident than that for greater identification with the people's interests. The unprecedented creation of an elite corps of some 100,000 cadres loyal to Gheorghiu-Dej, whose alleged function was to collaborate with the leading party organs for the proper execu-

[5] A comprehensive and enlightened discussion of these problems may be found in Ghita Ionescu, *Communism in Rumania: 1944–1962* (London: Oxford University Press, 1964), pp. 219–229.

[6] *Rezoluții*, Vol. II, pp. 451–470.

tion of the provisions of the Decision, occurred only after the leadership was unable to block a move by provincial delegates and a substantial segment of the Central Committee, headed by Constantinescu and Chişinevski, to convene the statutory party congress in 1954. The prospect of a congress meeting under uncertain circumstances undoubtedly spurred Gheorghiu-Dej's reassertion of the party's role as executor of the people's interests first at the plenum itself and more explicitly on the occasion of the ninth anniversary of Rumania's liberation. On August 23, 1953 two fundamental concepts of embryonic "Communist nationalism" were clearly enunciated: the party was the democratic political organization of all Rumanians, and it was dedicated to the construction of socialism in the Rumanian People's Republic for the benefit of the Rumanian people. The party's historic goal and Rumania's national goal were proclaimed to be one and the same.[7] These statements in no way questioned the need for continued subservience to the Soviet Union, which was still hailed as the sole liberator in August 1944 of the Rumanian people. But it was evident that Gheorghiu-Dej was already apprehensive over the consequences of a possible *rapprochement* between Russia and the United States. His record of constant and vitriolic denunciation of the "Anglo-American imperialists" and terrorization of their "agents" in Rumania could have become a fatal liability if peaceful coexistence were achieved. To atone for his past sins and to exonerate himself as best he could, Gheorghiu-Dej assumed the pose of champion of "peace and friendship among all peoples" in sponsoring the Fourth World Youth Festival that summer. Nevertheless, even as promoter of peace and supporter of all *démarches* for improvement of East-West relations, he unfailingly reiterated the irreversibility of Rumania's new political order. And as Russia's domestic and foreign policies continued to deviate from Stalinist norms, his fears mounted. Consequently, he began to reinforce the old and seek new anchors of support. He addressed himself more and more to the Rumanian people as the patriarchal protector of their interests and as the guide in the common struggle of building a prosperous socialist fatherland. He formally reasserted the party's leadership in the armed uprising of August 1944 on the occasion of the tenth anniversary of that event.[8] He even sought to reduce Rumania's exclusive economic and political dependence on the Soviet Union through repurchasing of Russian interests in the *Sovroms* and estab-

7 Complete text of Gheorghiu-Dej's speech, *Scînteia*, August 23, 1953.
8 *Ibid.*

lishing closer relations with China and Yugoslavia. But at all times he professed his devotion to the principles of Marxism-Leninism, jeopardized, by implication, by "deviationists," Russian and Rumanian.

It has been argued that Gheorghiu-Dej's Stalinist nationalism was the logical and inevitable synthesis of his Stalinism and the party's historic program for the "socialist transformation of Rumania." Accurate as this contention may be, it is evident that the synthesis was accelerated if not actually forced upon him by the activities of the new rulers in the Kremlin. The separation of functions between party and government and the corollary institution of collective leadership in the Soviet Union had to be emulated by the satellites early in 1954. This externally imposed and politically debilitating order faced Gheorghiu-Dej and his supporters with a major political threat at a time when his control of the party had not yet been consolidated. It was unwelcome per se as interference in Rumania's internal affairs but was particularly objectionable because the "revisionists" in the Kremlin had already approved the rehabilitation of several purged leaders in Eastern Europe and could conceivably have requested the exoneration and reinstatement of Pauker, Luca, Georgescu, or even Pătrăşcanu. To prevent any usurpation of his power during the period of dual rule, Gheorghiu-Dej took several characteristic precautionary measures. He had Pătrăşcanu executed, downgraded Constantinescu and Chişinevski, postponed the meeting of the party congress, and placed himself under the protective umbrella of the Stalinists in the Kremlin and the nationalists of the Chinese Communist Party.[9]

The significance of these actions, particularly the search for a Chinese crutch, has been until very recently inadequately recognized or grossly underestimated. Pătrăşcanu's summary trial and execution in April 1954 occurred only a few days before the installation of collective leadership in Rumania. Whether Pătrăşcanu could have become Khrushchev's man, as has been suggested, is difficult to ascertain. But Gheorghiu-Dej was not prepared to wait for future developments. With Pătrăşcanu removed, it was somewhat easier for him to accept the Russian-dictated reshuffling. It is noteworthy, however, that in the process of relinquishing the post of Secretary-General of the party and the establishment of a collective four-man Secretariat, he was able to prevent the inclusion

9 *Ibid.*, 1954, *passim.*

of Chişinevski and Constantinescu in that body. Instead, Gheorghe Apostol became First Secretary, and Nicolae Ceauşescu, Mihai Dalea and Ianoş Fazekaş secretaries.[10] The appointment of Ceauşescu, the leading political officer in the armed forces and one of Gheorghiu-Dej's foremost protégés, strengthened the Rumanian contingent particularly as he was also promoted to the post of candidate-member of the Politburo. Another rising star, Minister of Internal Affairs Alexandru Drăghici, joined Ceauşescu in the latter capacity. To prevent any possible reversal of these decisions by a general party assembly, Gheorghiu-Dej, by virtue of the strength he commanded in the top party echelons, secured the postponement of the congress until October. During these months he accelerated the process of building bridges with Peking and purging the party cadres of non-Stalinists.[11]

Although the evidence of contacts between the Rumanian and Chinese parties is conclusive, the nature of the relations is not always clear. Certain generalizations may nevertheless be made. From as early as February 1954 Gheorghiu-Dej regarded the concessions obtained by Peking from Moscow as worthy of emulation. On February 14 the view was expressed that the principles governing Sino-Soviet relations—"complete equality of rights, mutual respect of national interests, a common desire for peace"—should set the pattern for the entire socialist camp. This formula was repeated in the official Rumanian declaration concerning the Geneva Conference on Indochina issued on August 1 and again on the occasion of the celebration of Rumania's liberation on August 23.[12] That the Chinese responded favorably to this recognition of their status vis-à-vis the Soviet Union and consequent influence in the socialist world was strikingly evident in the congratulatory message sent by Mao Tse-tung and Chou En-lai to Gheorghiu-Dej on August 23. The Chinese alone of all Communist regimes took exception to the view that the Soviet armies had liberated Rumania. Instead, they credited the Rumanian Workers' Party, the unquestioned leader of the Rumanian people, with that patriotic action.[13] The Chinese thus endorsed Gheorghiu-Dej's daring reassertion of the party's role as coliberator and lent support to the Rumanians' nationalist proclivities. Gheorghiu-Dej quickly responded to the Chinese mes-

10 *Ibid.*, April 21, 1954.
11 Much insight into Gheorghiu-Dej's tactics may be gained from reading his speech "For the Continuing Strengthening of Party Work," *ibid.*, April 20, 1954.
12 *Ibid.*, February 14, August 1, and August 23, 1954.
13 *Ibid.*, August 23, 1954.

sage by publicly linking China's and Rumania's interest in the promotion of relations based on the Sino-Soviet formula. To emphasize the common bonds the Rumanians also pointed to the concurrent dissolution of the joint Russo-Rumanian (*Sovroms*) and Russo-Chinese mixed companies in September and October 1954.[14] Finally, in November Apostol made the Soviet formula on peaceful coexistence among countries with differing social and political systems—"respect for the principles of equality of rights and noninterference in the internal affairs of other countries"—applicable to Rumanian international relations in general and invoked the Sino-Indian statement on coexistence of June 1954 as the prototype for these international relations of "the new type."[15]

Whether the contacts between the Rumanians and the Chinese were more extensive than this brief review would indicate, or whether there was an organic link between the dissolution of the *Sovroms* and the parallel Sino-Soviet negotiations, is unknown. What is known, however, is that the constant invocation of Chinese actions and examples appeared in the Rumanian press side by side with reiteration of loyalty to the Soviet Union and Stalin, and that a concurrent Rumanian nationalist Stalinist course seeking independence in the conduct of internal affairs was evolving. Of course, the Russians may have been prepared to substitute less crude but equally effective means for the exploitation of the Rumanian economy than the *Sovroms*. On the other hand, the duration of the negotiations—more than six months—and the retention of interests in the key oil company, Sovrompetrol, are indicative of certain complications. It is also noteworthy that the negotiations were conducted by Miron Constantinescu, who was politically closer to the new Soviet leaders than Gheorghiu-Dej, and that he was removed from the Secretariat after the signing of the first dissolution agreement in February. It is improbable that the delays in the negotiations could be ascribed to Russian displeasure over Constantinescu's downgrading or that their successful conclusion was a political action designed to strengthen Constantinescu's position in relation to Gheorghiu-Dej's. However, in the fall of 1954 there is evidence that all was not well between the anti-Stalinists in the Kremlin and the Rumanian leadership and between Constantinescu and Gheorghiu-Dej. Constantinescu's eclipse continued even after the successful conclusion of the negotiations. He was impotent to prevent the second postponement of the congress and stood by help-

14 *Ibid.*, September 22–27 and October 13, 1954.
15 *Ibid.*, November 7, 1954.

lessly as Gheorghiu-Dej secured the belated conviction to life imprisonment of Vasile Luca.[16] Gheorghiu-Dej's actions were justified either directly or by implication in terms of the still-unrepaired damage caused by deviationists from the party line and Stalinist principles. They were also accompanied by pointed reiteration of the correctness of the party's historic policies, wholesale citations from the proceedings of the fifth anniversary of the establishment of the Chinese People's Republic, and constant publicizing of the principles championed by Russia and China—"equality of rights, noninterference in internal affairs, mutual respect of national interests."[17] The intensification of pro-Chinese statements in the winter and spring of 1955 reflects Gheorghiu-Dej's awareness of the concessions wrested by Peking from Khrushchev in October and attests to the strategic value he assigned to the Chinese in his own maneuvers for political consolidation. On the other hand, the Rumanian leader realized that Khrushchev's own position had been strengthened following the meetings with Mao Tse-tung and that it was therefore important to mend his fences with the Russians. As 1954 was drawing to a close, Gheorghiu-Dej's policy was evolving more and more into one of development of the national economy and assertion of Rumania's independence in domestic affairs and of diversification of external contacts as compatible with the policies of the Soviet Union. And this drive for greater national and international identification gained momentum in 1955.

It has generally been assumed that the intensification of Rumanian activity in foreign affairs recorded in 1954 and 1955 was part of a common pattern devised by the Kremlin for all its satellites. Upon closer examination, however, it is evident that the several economic and cultural agreements concluded by Rumania with Communist and non-Communist countries—particularly Yugoslavia, China, and France—were specifically designed to lessen Rumania's economic and political dependence on Russia and thus to strengthen Gheorghiu-Dej's bargaining power with Moscow. The Rumanian overtures toward Yugoslavia, antedating the Russian, did not necessarily reflect Moscow's wishes and instructions. It is true that the initial moves, starting with the reopening of railroad traffic between the two countries in October 1954 and continuing with growing intensity throughout the months preceding Krush-

---

16 *Ibid.*, October 10, 28, 1954.
17 *Ibid.*, October 13–28, 1954.

chev's and Bulganin's visit to Belgrade in May 1955, were made in anticipation of a Russo-Yugoslav reconciliation. But as explicitly stated in December 1954, Gheorghiu-Dej's immediate aim was to precipitate formal acceptance by Moscow of the extension of the principles governing Sino-Soviet relations to all members of the socialist community.[18] Similarly, the renewal of economic and cultural ties with France in the winter of 1954–1955 was intended to exploit Russia's readiness to improve relations with the West to his own advantage.[19] Evidently, Gheorghiu-Dej sought to limit Russia's self-assigned role of exclusive spokesman for the bloc and thus to prevent a priori commitment to policies that could affect adversely his, and by extension Rumania's, interests. Yet he readily supported Russian policies and actions designed to limit possible interference by the West in Rumanian affairs. He was an enthusiastic supporter of the Warsaw Pact and the first to subscribe, in 1955, to Khrushchev's view that the provisions of the peace treaty with Rumania requiring withdrawal of Soviet troops following the conclusion of the treaty with Austria had been invalidated by the establishment of NATO.[20]

The dual attitude toward Moscow was much less evident in internal affairs, where Gheorghiu-Dej sought total freedom from Russian interference even though in the last analysis his regime's ultimate survival depended on Russian support. But his public warning to Khrushchev on the occasion of the eleventh anniversary of the country's liberation that Rumania would not tolerate interference in its internal affairs from anyone was realistically conceived in terms of his own group's strength, fears, and interests.[21] Strength, such as it was, was derived from consolidation of Gheorghiu-Dej's position in the Rumanian party and the country at large. The building of the special *aktiv* continued apace with constant purges of sympathizers of the "antiparty" group and enrollment of industrial workers. Termination of rationing, enactment of price reductions, liberation of certain political prisoners, re-establishment of contacts with the West, and endorsement of international coexistence created an atmosphere more favorable to

[18] Much is said directly and even more by implication in Gheorghiu-Dej's statements to Yugoslav press correspondents, *ibid.*, December 31, 1954.

[19] *Ibid.*, December 26, 1954.

[20] See Gheorghiu-Dej's interview with A. L. Bradford of the United Press in *ibid.*, August 26, 1955.

[21] The far-reaching statements contained in Gheorghiu-Dej's speech on the occasion of the eleventh anniversary of Rumania's liberation have been generally overlooked by students of Rumanian affairs. Complete text in *ibid.*, August 23, 1955.

acceptance of the party line. The reassertion of the party's primacy in formulation of the actions and policies that led to the country's liberation in 1944, still in conjunction with the Russian armies, and the steady improvement of Rumanian conditions ever since seemed more plausible in August 1955 than at any time previously.[22] On the other hand, Gheorghiu-Dej remained identified with Stalinism in Rumania as well as in Moscow, and his proclaimed policy of independence in the conduct of internal affairs was less than palatable to Khrushchev even if offset by a statement of acceptance of Russia's leadership of the socialist camp and of support for Moscow's foreign policy. It is noteworthy that in his own speech on August 23 Khrushchev failed to take notice of Gheorghiu-Dej's key points regarding the role played by the Rumanian party in the liberation and subsequent socialist construction and of the universal applicability of the principles embodied in international relations of "the new type" beyond recognizing the Rumanians' progress and achievements in the common cause. Moreover, his preferences for closer adherence to the principles of collective leadership, diminution of Gheorghiu-Dej's power, and strengthening of Constantinescu's and Chişinevski's positions were implied in the speech and later confirmed by Rumanian and Russian actions and statements.[23] In August 1955, however, Khrushchev agreed grudgingly that Gheorghiu-Dej's policies were not sufficiently incompatible with Russia's interests to deny Gheorghiu-Dej's primacy in the Rumanian party and to endorse his plans for socialist construction. The mutual recognition that Russo-Rumanian relations were in fact different from what they had been in Stalin's days of total subservience did not represent a complete reconciliation of Gheorghiu-Dej's and Khrushchev's interests. Gheorghiu-Dej was too Stalinist and independent for Khrushchev's plans and comfort, and Khrushchev was too willing to cooperate with the West and generally too much of a "revisionist" for Gheorghiu-Dej's. Having, however, exposed their separate views on August 23 and established the basis for coexistence still primarily *à la Russe*, Gheorghiu-Dej proceeded to call the party congress for December 1955. Prior to the meeting he reassumed the position of First Secretary, removed Constantinescu from command of the State Planning Commission, and appointed his right-hand man, Chivu Stoica, to the presidency of the Council of Ministers.[24] On December 28, as

---

22 *Ibid.*
23 Khrushchev's speech also in *ibid.*, August 23, 1955.
24 *Ibid.*, October 4, 1955.

the Second Congress ended, Gheorghiu-Dej emerged as the undisputed leader of a Rumanian Workers' Party dedicated to the attainment of its historic goals primarily à la Gheorghiu-Dej.

The significance of the Second Congress has been generally underestimated by contemporary observers and later students of Rumanian communism. The tendency to stress the weakness of the party and subservience to Russia—viewed as an indispensable protector and source of economic support—has obscured the importance of political measures, recommended by Gheorghiu-Dej and adopted by the congress, that were designed to reduce Rumania's dependence on the Soviet Union. Whether Gheorghiu-Dej had any inkling of Khrushchev's specific line of attack on Stalinism at the time of the December meeting is unknown. But it is evident that his awareness of the Russian leader's anti-Stalinism had increased after Khrushchev's visit to Rumania in August 1955 and that the necessary adjustments and fortifications, at home and abroad, had to be made in anticipation of further "liberalization" by the Kremlin. It has become clear that the currently heralded "independent" Rumanian policies were tentatively formulated in Gheorghiu-Dej's report on the activities of the Central Committee.[25] Then, for the first time, he explicitly affirmed the need for adapting Marxist-Leninist principles to the specific national interests and problems of Rumania, equated with the attainment of socialism on blueprints traced by the party in 1945. The socialist transformation of Rumania, he stated, would not be subordinated to but rather harmoniously blended with the interests of the socialist camp headed by the Soviet Union. The principles of interaction between socialist patriotism and proletarian internationalism "according to each people's wishes and interests," on the basis of the correct intercamp and international relations of "respect of national sovereignty and equality of rights, nonaggression, and peaceful settlement of all problems, peaceful coexistence among countries with different social systems, and noninterference in internal affairs," were expressly invoked in support of his thesis. In pragmatic political terms Gheorghiu-Dej sought and obtained a clear mandate for himself and trusted members of his team for the attainment of the historic goals of the party: his own political survival and Ru-

[25] Gheorghe Gheorghiu-Dej, *Raportul de activitate al comitetului central al Partidului Muncitoresc Romîn la congresul al II-lea al partidului* [Report of the Central Committee of the Rumanian Workers' Party at the Second Party Congress] (Bucharest: Editura de Stat Pentru Literatură Politică, 1956), pp. 5–160. (Hereinafter cited as *Raportul*).

mania's socialist transformation. The course chosen was in turn characterized by rigidity in domestic affairs and flexibility in foreign.

The tightening of Gheorghiu-Dej's control over the party organization at both the central and regional-local levels was his greatest achievement in December 1955. Even if the party itself was smaller than in 1948 and still composed predominantly of men recruited by Pauker and Constantinescu, the leading cadres and the *aktiv* established in 1953 consisted of individuals hand-picked by Gheorghiu-Dej. His most striking accomplishment was the packing of the Central Committee, Politburo, and Secretariat with as many of his men as possible and the removal from key posts of potential rivals suspected of "liberalism." The Central Committee was enlarged through the inclusion as members or candidate-members of reliable regional first secretaries. The downgrading from the rank of full to that of candidate-member of Ion Gheorghe Maurer, the present Rumanian premier, and Gheorghe Vasilichi, a non-Stalinist connected with the railway workers and with Pătrășcanu, was characteristic of Gheorghiu-Dej's political caution. It was, however, less significant than the promotion of Nicolae Ceaușescu and Alexandru Drăghici to the Politburo and certainly less so than Constantinescu's official demotion to the seventh position in that twelve-man body. Despite these successful maneuvers Gheorghiu-Dej remained apprehensive over the inadequate social composition of the party and the survival of individuals and tendencies associated with the right-wing deviationists. His stern call for increased party discipline, revolutionary vigilance, and continuation of the class struggle was reminiscent of the darkest Stalinist days. It was unequivocally directed against all those within and without the party who hoped that the relaxation of international tensions and the advent of Khrushchev would result in "liberalization" or even "liberation" from communism.[26]

His apprehensions, even if magnified for tactical purposes, were not totally unfounded. The majority of the population was still clearly opposed to communism in 1955, and its national goal remained Gheorghiu-Dej's removal from power rather than the attainment of socialism under his leadership. Even if the number of those who expected "liberation" by the West was small and restricted to the decimated bourgeoisie and aristocracy, a few intellectuals, kulaks, and professional cadres, hope for "liberalization" of the Communist order was rising throughout the country. As

26 A convenient summary of the proceedings of the Second Congress may be found in Ionescu, *Communism in Rumania*, pp. 240–247.

liberalization posed the risk of his replacement by men less identified with Stalin, Gheorghiu-Dej propounded the alternate formulas of "socialist patriotism" and party paternalism, both designed to convey the image of himself as architect of the country's "national" and "social" liberation in 1944 and Rumania's subsequent and future progress.[27] By implication he also sought to alter the popular image of him as a Moscovite agent by depicting himself as a Communist leader acting in terms of specific Rumanian conditions. This disassociation from Russia seemed essential not so much because Khrushchevism was more popular than his own brand of communism but essentially because his formulas for political survival and socialist construction required an economy not fully dependent on Russian support and a political order not subject to interference from Moscow. That such were his intentions is also evident from his reiteration at the congress of Rumania's achievements in international affairs: expansion of diplomatic and trade relations with nonmembers of the Soviet bloc, strengthening of relations with China and Yugoslavia, and admission to the United Nations.[28] These statements were designed to emphasize the establishment of a stronger basis for national identification, wider recognition of the legitimacy of his regime, and support for the attainment of his goals and, ultimately, to provide him with greater leverage against Khrushchev. All told, in December 1955 Gheorghiu-Dej formally assigned to the party the role of executor of the country's historic legacy—the attainment of a prosperous and independent socialist Rumania—and committed himself to the execution of that task according to plans formulated at the party conference in 1945 and reformulated ten years later.

The elements of safety contained in the line enunciated and political actions taken by Gheorghiu-Dej in December were sufficient for him to weather the storm generated by Khrushchev's denunciation of Stalin and the "revisionist" program and policies adopted at the Soviet Communist Party's Twentieth Congress in February 1956. In principle, Khrushchev's call for de-Stalinization, condemnation of the cult of personality and one-man rule, request for democratization of the party and governmental processes and firm adherence to the principles of collective leadership, and proposals for increased coordination of the economies of the bloc coun-

[27] On these points consult Stephen Fischer-Galati, ed., *Romania* (New York: Praeger, 1957), pp. 60–181.
[28] Gheorghiu-Dej, *Raportul*, pp. 5–20.

tries through the CMEA (Council for Mutual Economic Aid) ran counter to Gheorghiu-Dej's policies and methods. In practice, however, although squarely opposed to collective leadership, de-Stalinization, and expansion of Soviet control over the Rumanian economy through CMEA, Gheorghiu-Dej was able to make the adjustments required to overcome all threats to his supremacy and to emerge in a stronger position at the end of a protracted struggle for power with the "liberals." Whether Gheorghiu-Dej was afraid of direct intervention by Moscow in Rumanian affairs to remove Stalinists from the party elite is a matter of speculation. It is clear, however, that even if he excluded that possibility in 1956—as he apparently did—he feared indirect pressure from Moscow and on that basis proceeded to strengthen his ties with all who could reinforce his own position and political line and thus hold at bay all actual or potential challengers.

With characteristic tactical flexibility Gheorghiu-Dej tried to prove that the Rumanian line was not per se incompatible with Khrushchev's general precepts, that it was in fact an adaptation of the universally true Marxist-Leninist principles to specific Rumanian conditions. If Khrushchevism was a correct derivative of Marxism-Leninism for Russia—which he did not necessarily concede—Gheorghiu-Dejism was unquestionably the Rumanian counterpart to Khrushchevism. Stalinism too had been a correct adaptation of Marxism-Leninism to specific Russian, and even Rumanian, conditions, but the principles of the basic Communist doctrine were abused by the late dictator who failed to take into account the changing conditions in Russia and the Communist world. Gheorghiu-Dej, however, never committed the sins of which Stalin was accused, for he was always aware of Rumanian conditions and Marxist-Leninist precepts and invariably condemned deviations of all kinds. This, he argued in his lengthy account to the party's Central Committee dedicated to the proceedings of the Twentieth Congress, was evident from the history of the party, its programs, plans, and achievements, and its intolerance toward the "antiparty" group headed by Ana Pauker and Vasile Luca. Gheorghiu-Dej and his close associates had always believed in collective leadership, albeit Stalinist since such was required in Rumania, and if they had been unable to exercise these principles, it was because of Pauker's and Luca's championing and arrogating to themselves the "cult of personality."[29] In sum, then, he and his associates were the

29 *Scinteia*, March 29, 1956.

best judges of what was appropriate for Rumania as both true Marxist-Leninists and Rumanian "patriotic socialists." The reiteration of the current doctrines, minimally adapted to Khrushchev's views but in fact in opposition to them, was possible only because Gheorghiu-Dej apparently felt sufficiently secure from damaging internal and external pressures. It is indeed noteworthy that the challenge to his interpretation of Khrushchev's message set forth at the meeting of the Central Committee by Iosif Chişinevski and Miron Constantinescu was successfully rebuffed by Gheorghiu-Dej and his supporters.[30]

The significance of Chişinevski's and Constantinescu's actions has not been fully appreciated by contemporary or later students of the events of 1956. Chişinevski's demand for liberalization and his rejection of Gheorghiu-Dej's rationalizations were only superficially comparable to the similar views expressed by Constantinescu. Chişinevski was the highest nonaccredited representative of the Kremlin in the Rumanian bureaucracy. His role as the link between the Russian and Rumanian apparatus was maintained at various levels of the Rumanian party machinery since the ousting of Pauker and Luca, and his presence in the upper echelons was desired by the Kremlin and, *à faute de mieux*, accepted by Gheorghiu-Dej. Chişinevski, by virtue of his ethnic, professional, and religious background, could not and did not aspire to assume the leadership of the party but acted merely as a watchdog for the Russian interests of the moment. His challenge to Gheorghiu-Dej in March 1956 was on behalf of Khrushchev and in conjunction with Constantinescu's. Constantinescu, on the other hand, was the only leading Rumanian Communist who could have replaced Gheorghiu-Dej in 1956. Ideologically he was clearly closer to Khrushchev than was Gheorghiu-Dej, and he had the advantage of identification with the rank and file of the party. It is evident that Constantinescu's move at the meeting was designed not to oust Gheorghiu-Dej but to obtain the support of the Central Committee for "liberalization" and to secure his own elevation in the ranks of the power elite. With Chişinevski's assistance and presumably Khrushchev's blessings, if not direct support, the balance of power in the Central Committee might have been altered in a manner that would eventually have brought about the political

[30] The confrontation between Gheorghiu-Dej and Constantinescu and Chişinevski became known only in July 1957. Details were then provided by Gheorghiu-Dej and supplementary data made available in 1961. See footnote 2. Consult also Ionescu, *Communism in Rumania*, pp. 259–262.

demise of Gheorghiu-Dej and his team. The exact details of the proceedings of the meeting of March 1956 are not known; but shortly thereafter Chişinevski went into prolonged and Constantinescu into temporary obscurity, while Gheorghiu-Dej reaffirmed the correctness of his policies with increasingly greater vigor and acted accordingly.

On the basis of the available evidence it is apparent that even though Constantinescu and Chişinevski did not command a majority in the Central Committee and, clearly, the unconditional support of the Kremlin, their demands for liberalization could not be altogether ignored.[31] Gheorghiu-Dej was, however, able to circumvent the Khrushchevite message in the Constantinescu-Chişinevski interpretation by substituting the concept of what may be described as "technical liberalization" within a basically Stalinist framework. While he remained adamantly opposed to removal of the stranglehold imposed upon intellectual expression and ruthlessly purged all "deviationists" from socialist realism in arts and letters, he allowed the technocrats and intellectuals of "unhealthy" social origin to rejoin the country's professional cadres. Anyone prepared to substitute "socialist patriotism" for the violently condemned "bourgeois nationalism" and to dedicate himself to the "socialist transformation of Rumania" per se and for the ultimate strengthening of the socialist camp was welcomed as long as he accepted the dictates and program of the party and Gheorghiu-Dej's line.[32] To Gheorghiu-Dej and his closest associates, liberalization meant merely the granting of such concessions as seemed essential for the attainment of his economic and political goals, but under no circumstance did it mean toleration of any trends, social, economic, or intellectual, that could in the least permit the fusion of forces seeking "liberalization" according to formulas not "germane to Rumanian conditions." The extent to which this line (and implementing measures) could have been successfully pursued had it not been for the ill-fated Hungarian Revolution of October 1956 is a matter of debate. However, it was accepted by the majority of the Central Committee in March 1956 and rigorously pursued until the Hungarian debacle, when its validity was recognized

[31] It is now assumed that Gheorghiu-Dej did not command the unequivocal support of the present Rumanian leadership in 1956. The rehabilitation of Constantinescu following Gheorghiu-Dej's death and the implicit condemnation of Gheorghiu's methods would tend to support the contention that Constantinescu's views were tacitly shared by Ceauşescu and other members of his team.

[32] A very illuminating discussion can be found in Ionescu, *Communism in Rumania*, pp. 262–266.

even by Khrushchev. The extent of its acceptance by the minority of the Central Committee, by Constantinescu and Chişinevski, by the rank and file of the party and the population, and by Khrushchev himself before November 1956 is much less certain. Gheorghiu-Dej's constant call for increased party discipline and revolutionary vigilance, his unequivocal condemnation of "deviations" and "deviationists" past and present, and his increasingly more precise reiteration of each country's right to pursue its internal and foreign policies according to specific national conditions and on the basis of the principles of "mutual respect for sovereignty and territorial integrity and noninterference in other countries' internal affairs" attest if not to political insecurity at least to the need for consolidation of his position against damaging actions. Significantly, between March and October Gheorghiu-Dej appeared particularly concerned with the attitude of the intellectuals and youth at home and with consolidation of his ties with Yugoslavia, China, and even the West abroad. His domestic worries stemmed less from any strength that the writers or artists enjoyed by themselves or the extent to which the young people could be influenced by exposure to less dogmatic intellectual manifestations than by the fear that Constantinescu, a young intellectual himself, could become the rallying point of those seeking liberalization. It was not by coincidence that Gheorghiu-Dej's condemnation of intellectual liberalism and warnings to the Union of Working Youth concerning inadequate execution of the directives of the Second Congress and Constantinescu's virtual disappearance from public life all occurred within a period of two weeks after the termination of Tito's visit to Moscow and one week after Tito's visit to Bucharest.[33] The evidence would indicate that Gheorghiu-Dej's actions were, in effect, a reaction to joint Russo-Yugoslav pressures for liberalization, which he was able partially to circumvent by reinterpretation of the letter and spirit of the principles guiding the Soviet-Yugoslav agreement of June 1956. This interpretation is supported by the fact that Miron Constantinescu, who held most of the conversations with Tito during the Yugoslav leader's stopover en route to Moscow early in June, and who voiced views fully comparable to Tito's and Khrushchev's at that time, was conspicuously absent during the return visit.[34] The final communiqué itself, issued on June 27, revealed distinct divergences between the Yugo-

[33] The dramatic sequence of events and statements of June 1956 is faithfully recorded in *Scînteia*, June 24–27, 1956.

[34] *Ibid.*, June 2, 1956.

slav and Rumanian interpretation of the mandate of the Twentieth Congress, the Yugoslav position being much closer to Khrushchev's than the Rumanian.[35] Significantly, the Rumanian position, made even more explicit in a *Scînteia* editorial, emphasized the elements of Titoism that best suited Gheorghiu-Dej's purposes: independence in the conduct of domestic affairs, based on specific national characteristics and historic conditions, and general applicability of the principles of "relations of the new type" in international affairs.[36] The all-important concept that the construction of socialism may vary in different countries depending on specific circumstances, put forth then and reiterated just as forcefully on the occasion of Gheorghiu-Dej's return visit to Yugoslavia in October, was clearly designed to defend Gheorghiu-Dejism and to limit external influences and pressures for changes incompatible with Rumanian objective conditions, best equated with any threats to his own power.[37] It was also in this spirit and in accordance with these principles that he personally offered to settle all outstanding issues with the United States on July 4.[38] And the reiteration of the same themes during his memorable speech to the Eighth Congress of the Chinese Communist Party in September and in all other official pronunciamentos on international affairs during the spring, summer, and early fall of 1956 attests to his concern for acceptance of his line by "revisionists" of all kinds.[39]

The events in Poland and Hungary in October and even the limited expressions of discontent registered in Rumania during the Hungarian Revolution proved that his diagnosis of Rumanian conditions was accurate and that his policies were largely justified. Whether the revolution would have spilled over into Rumania had the Russians chosen a course different from armed intervention in Hungary is still a matter of dispute among experts.[40] Similarly, the question of the form such an anti-Communist movement would have assumed is also a matter of speculation. On the basis of the evidence available it is probable that revolutionary manifestations, short of a total collapse of the Communist order in Hungary, would have been limited in scope and would have involved ele-

---

35 *Ibid.*, June 27, 1956.

36 See editorial "Bine aţi venit dragi oaspeţi iugoslavi!" [Welcome Dear Yugoslav Guests!], *ibid.*, June 24, 1956.

37 *Ibid.*, October 21, 23, 1956.

38 *Ibid.*, July 5, 1956.

39 *Ibid.*, September 19, 1956.

40 A review of these problems may be found in Ionescu, *Communism in Rumania*, pp. 267–287.

ments other than the "class enemy." In fact, the most striking phenomenon in the few demonstrations and expressions of discontent recorded in Rumania during the first days of the Hungarian uprising is that they occurred among students and industrial workers and reflected dissatisfaction with economic conditions and anti-Russian grievances. No calls for the overthrow of the Communist regime per se were voiced at any time. By contrast, those most suspect to the regime, the discontented peasantry, the intellectuals, and all inhabitants of "bourgeois" or "aristocratic" origin, remained strictly on the sidelines, possibly (but by no means certainly) awaiting "liberation" or "liberalization." It is evident that the repressive measures utilized so effectively by Gheorghiu-Dej prior to the events of October 1956, as well as the party's constant refusal to allow any meaningful "liberalization" after the Russian Twentieth Congress, were far more responsible for the passivity of the Rumanians than acceptance of the "nationalistic" political doctrine enunciated by the leadership or the hurried economic concessions and promises made at the height of the Hungarian crisis.[41] On the other hand, the anti-Russian character of the students' manifestations, concentrating on cessation of subservience to Russia and of Russian interference in Rumanian affairs, and of the workers' demands for more favorable working conditions and higher wages—apparently impossible because of Russian economic exploitation—did represent recognition and partial acceptance of Gheorghiu-Dejism. They were not a rejection of its principles but rather a demand that they be carried to the logical, anti-Russian, conclusion.

However encouraging these Rumanian developments may have been to Gheorghiu-Dej, he knew that his political survival was due to Russia's intervention in Hungary. Even if the forces of "liberation" did not show their hand, it is clear that they would have done so either directly in the event of a major upheaval or, had Nagy survived politically, in conjunction with those favoring "liberalization." The student manifestations, particularly those involving the Hungarian youth in Transylvania, were, after all, indicative of "liberal" if not "bourgeois nationalist" or even "chauvinist" intellectual ferment and, like the workers' demands, reflected a grave lack of Communist discipline. Nevertheless, while these deficiencies had to be "corrected," it is evident that Gheorghiu-Dej was sufficiently reassured by the reaction of the Rumanians—as well as of Russia and the West—to the Hungarian Revolution to adhere to

41 *Scînteia,* October 30, 1956.

his basic doctrinal tenets and to expand them in scope and depth in a manner commensurate with his political safety.

Many of the misconceptions regarding the evolution of the Rumanian course can be traced directly to misinterpretation of the party's reaction to the events of 1956. The most common view, that Gheorghiu-Dej reconciled his differences with Khrushchev as soon as Khrushchev assumed a Stalinist posture after the Hungarian uprising and that this *rapprochement* was the result of common fears of "counterrevolution" and "imperialist aggression," represents a gross oversimplification of complex issues.[42] An analysis of official documents and statements of the fateful months from October 1956 to July 1957 reveals that this *rapprochement* was superficial since the differences between the Rumanian and Russian leaders were too marked to allow anything beyond temporary reconciliation.

The Rumanian leaders, like most Rumanians, realized that the possibility of "liberation" by the West and of successful "counterrevolution" virtually ended with the Hungarian debacle. Under such circumstances, the Rumanian security and police forces alone could ensure order in the country; the *raison d'être* of the Russian troops in Rumania had *de facto* ended. The Russian armies, a source of potential interference with the execution of plans for the socialist transformation of Rumania, were *de trop*. The Rumanians were also aware that the gains made by Tito, Mao, and Gomułka were not nullified by the events in Hungary and apparently were not anxious to relinquish their own. Gheorghiu-Dej was not interested in becoming a Kádár in the fall of 1956, nor did he seek reconciliation with Khrushchev for the resurrection of Stalinism. Instead he sought to obtain the Russians' support for Gheorghiu-Dejism, which itself assumed a more pronounced anti-Russian character after Moscow's refusal fully to endorse its tenets in December 1956.[43]

Whether the decision to pursue a policy of "national unification" in the spirit of "socialist patriotism" rather than of repression of the students guilty of "bourgeois nationalism" and of the "class enemy" suspected of entertaining similar sentiments was initially

42 See footnote 40.

43 The divergences between Moscow and Bucharest are clearly illustrated in the joint declaration on the negotiations held in Moscow between November 26 and December 3, 1956, published in an English version in *Soviet News,* December 4, 1956.

Gheorghiu-Dej's or was accepted by him under pressure from the "liberals" in the party is unknown. But the appointment of Constantinescu as Minister of Culture and Education during the Hungarian Revolution, the abolition of the compulsory teaching of Russian in universities, and the subsequent call for mass endorsement of the party's program and principles issued by the Communist leadership would indicate the existence of a basic consensus on the pursuit of a "Rumanian road to socialism." The proposals submitted by the Rumanian delegation to Moscow in December, in connection with the general reviewing of Soviet-Rumanian political and economic relations, in effect demanded compliance with the terms of Moscow's own "Declaration on the Principles of Development and Further Strengthening of Friendship and Cooperation between the Soviet Union and other Socialist States" issued at the height of the Hungarian crisis. It is believed that, apart from the economic concessions requested, and partly received, the Rumanians sought formal recognition by the Kremlin of the continuing validity of the principles guiding "relations of the new type" between the two countries, Rumania's right to determine its own "road to socialism" within the socialist camp, and a definite commitment for the withdrawal of Russian troops. Moscow's response was evidently less satisfactory than expected. The economic provisions of the agreement, while favorable to the extent of facilitating Rumania's economic development, did not substantially reduce her economic dependence on Russia. Politically, however, the Kremlin refused the Rumanian demands except for readjustment of the legal status of the Russian armed forces in the country.[44]

The Rumanian reaction, far from that hitherto assumed of jubilation over the economic gains reaped in Moscow, was one of increased, if cautious, flirtation with Yugoslavia, China, Poland, and the West and the channeling of "bourgeois nationalism" into "socialist patriotism" at home. These responses were all the more significant as plans for intensification of socialist construction became possible subsequent to the economic agreements. But the policy of partial disengagement from Russia according to the revised post-Hungarian Revolution formula soon revealed serious contradictions within the party leadership itself. Whereas there apparently was full agreement on the implementation of economic measures de-

[44] An informative analysis is contained in Ionescu, *Communism in Rumania*, pp. 273–275.

signed to facilitate the attainment of the plans formulated at the Second Congress, on streamlining the governmental structure and limited decentralization, as well as on assertion of the validity of the principles guiding relations among socialist nations and international affairs in general, the problem of Rumania's position in the socialist camp and direction of its "deviation" from Stalinism and Khrushchevism assumed critical proportions by the summer of 1957.

Although the details of the conflict are not fully known, it is believed that the Rumanian policy of straddling the fence between the conflicting interpretations of Marxism-Leninism held by China, Poland, Yugoslavia, and the Soviet Union reached a crisis by May 1957. Gheorghiu-Dej, while realizing the inherent contradictions, sought to exploit them only to the extent of asserting Rumania's right constructively to apply the principles of Marxism-Leninism in accordance with specific Rumanian conditions. However, his concurrent attempt to bring the party's image as the executor of Rumania's national goal—the creation of a prosperous socialist country—into clearer focus had the effect of increasing the expectations of the party and population for greater detachment from the main "enemy," Russia, and emulation of the more "liberal" tendencies manifested by Gomułka, Tito, and Mao. Whether Gheorghiu-Dejism would have become more "nationalistic" and "liberal" as the differences between the Russian, Chinese, Yugoslav, and Polish positions sharpened in the spring of 1957 is a matter of speculation. The evidence is contradictory, but on balance it tends to indicate that Gheorghiu-Dej became increasingly more concerned with the "liberal" tendencies of Gomułka and the Chinese without, however, fully endorsing the conservative line emanating from the Kremlin. He found ideological solace in the "neo-Stalinist" umbrella provided by Moscow but remained leery of Russia's determination to avoid formal acceptance of the "relations of the new type" propounded by Gheorghiu-Dej. The determining factor in his restricting the scope of "Rumania's road to socialism," in June, was the removal of the threat to his political security and that of his ideologically conservative associates from "liberals" and "nationalists" within the party, headed by Miron Constantinescu.[45] The demands for "liberalization" of party policies

---

45 The evolution of Gheorghiu-Dej's attitudes and policies becomes most apparent from analyzing the contents of the several major speeches delivered between the December 1956 Plenum of the party's Central Committee and the purging of Constantinescu and Chişinevski during the Plenum of June 28–July

and "socialist re-education" of the masses voiced since November 1956 were apparently accepted by Gheorghiu-Dej until it became evident that Constantinescu's views were undercutting the authority of the conservatives in the party. Concern over "revisionism" became sufficiently marked by June, when a plenary session of the Central Committee was summoned to define the ideological tenets of Rumanian communism, in the light of developments since the party's Second and the Soviet Twentieth Congress.

It is not entirely clear whether the meeting that opened on June 28 accidentally coincided with that of the Soviet party's during which the antiparty group was removed from power by Khrushchev's forces or whether it was purposely scheduled for that date by the Rumanian "conservatives" or "liberals." But it is known that Constantinescu, supported by Chişinevski, attacked Gheorghiu-Dej as an ideological accomplice of the Russian "antiparty" group and sought the Central Committee's endorsement for the adoption of Khrushchevism à la Constantinescu. Apparently, his challenge was sufficiently effective to generate extensive debate but ineffectual in terms of its ultimate aim. On July 3 Gheorghiu-Dej's forces were able to purge Constantinescu and Chişinevski from the highest echelons of the party by reason of their "liberalism," "right-wing deviationism," "opportunism," and moves to undermine the ideological purity and discipline of the party. That Constantinescu's move was synchronized with the counteroffensive of the Khrushchev forces in Russia is certain; it is, however, doubtful that he acted on Khrushchev's instructions. Nevertheless, Constantinescu's linking of Gheorghiu-Dej with Molotov, Malenkov, and their confreres and Gheorghiu-Dej's rejection of the "deviationists'" demands affected Gheorghiu's relations with Moscow, with Constantinescu's supporters in the party, and with the Rumanian population at large.[46]

The crisis of July 1957 was ultimately concerned with the nature and direction of Rumanian "national communism." Gheorghiu-Dej's "nationalist" plans for limited disengagement from Moscow could not have failed to generate undesirable side effects. The line

3, 1957. These materials have been conveniently collected in Gheorghe Gheorghiu-Dej, *Articole şi cuvîntări, decembrie 1955–iulie 1959* [Articles and Speeches, December 1955–July 1959] (Bucharest: Editura Politică, 1959), pp. 208–305, hereafter cited as Gheorghiu-Dej, *Articole şi cuvîntări*.

46 *Scînteia*, July 9, 1957 provides the essential data that would support this composite interpretation of the events of June 28–July 3. See also footnotes 2, 30, and 31.

of demarcation between "socialist patriotism" and "socialist nationalism" was a thin one, as demonstrated in Poland, Yugoslavia, and China; and the three countries' interpretation of the principles of Marxism-Leninism resulted in syntheses much more liberal than those acceptable to the Rumanian power elite. Constantinescu's views provided a broader and more logical framework for the execution of the party's plans for Rumania's socialist transformation, in terms of the national goal of "socialist construction" and of the lessons of the Twentieth Congress, than was palatable to Gheorghiu-Dej. As long as Khrushchev was contained by opposing factions in the Kremlin, Gheorghiu-Dej could afford to experiment in Rumania. Khrushchev's victory and the corresponding challenge by the Rumanian "deviationists," however, presented the double danger of Russian support of Constantinescu and, the more serious and lasting one, of Khrushchevism. Constantinescu's dismissal removed the first but not the second.

Gheorghiu-Dej's reaction to Khrushchev's victory, as it evolved after July 1957, was closely related to his appraisal of the immediate and long-range threats posed by the Kremlin. The Rumanian leadership appeared determined to pursue policies of limited disengagement from Russia and promotion of its own schemes for Rumania's economic development. To attain this aim and resist Russian pressures, it sought to expand further and diversify the country's international relations, to secure the withdrawal of Russian troops, and to destroy all internal opposition to Gheorghiu-Dej's plans for the socialist transformation of Rumania. These objectives were entirely consistent with the attainment of the elite's immediate goal of consolidating its own power in Rumania and of enhancing that of their country in the socialist camp through careful exploitation of opportunities afforded by changing international conditions.

It would be difficult to demonstrate that the decisions reached at the crucial plenum of the party's Central Committee of November 1958, which formalized Gheorghiu-Dej's commitment to a Rumanian road to socialism, were tentatively formulated in July 1957. However, even a cursory review of the evidence tends to substantiate the thesis that, although the very form of the decisions of 1958 was not clear in 1957, their essence was contained in Gheorghiu-Dej's pragmatic political philosophy.[47] Characteristically, Gheorghiu-Dej

---

47 Compare Gheorghiu-Dej's speech at the November 1958 Plenum (*Scînteia*, December 2, 1958) with earlier statements starting with his article on the October Revolution (*Pravda*, October 29, 1957), all contained in Gheorghiu-Dej, *Articole şi cuvîntări*, pp. 317–584.

made two seemingly contradictory moves in July 1957: he appointed Ion Gheorghe Maurer as Minister of Foreign Affairs and issued a call for stringent persecution of those seeking to undermine the stability of the state through dissemination of bourgeois ideology and economic sabotage.[48] Maurer was elevated from the political obscurity to which he had been relegated because of "liberalism" in 1955 by Gheorghiu-Dej's own volition. This move was not designed to appease the Constantinescu wing or Khrushchev as is frequently assumed. Maurer's ascendancy, culminating in January 1958 with his replacing Groza as Chairman of the Presidium of the Grand National Assembly, was related to a major drive by Rumania for international recognition and assertion. Whether Maurer's ideas on "disengagement through diversification," which have earned him the reputation as coarchitect of the current Rumanian independent course, were influential in 1957 can only be surmised; in any event, they were known and presumably acceptable to Gheorghiu-Dej. During his brief term in office as Minister of Foreign Affairs and his longer one as Chairman of the Presidium, Rumanian policies closely followed the basic pattern with which he is currently identified.[49] The view that the Rumanians were acting merely as agents of Khrushchev in all political initiatives in 1957 and 1958 is not entirely correct; they did so only to the extent to which their own interests coincided with those of the Russians. The Stoica Plan for collaboration among all Balkan countries submitted in September did serve Russia's political purposes of the moment, but it also provided the Rumanians with an instrument for establishing their political respectability and for assuming a prominent role in enunciation of bloc policies.[50] On the other hand, subsequent major diplomatic actions, mostly after the November meeting of Communist parties in Moscow, were at best only superficially acceptable to Khrushchev. The Rumanians' endorsement of the Russian interpretation of the Moscow Declaration was by no means unconditional. The acceptance of Moscow's leadership of the socialist camp was not unequivocal; the Rumanians insisted on the equality of all members of the socialist community and strict application of the principles of noninterference and, in domestic affairs, observance of the rights of individual members, and all other guidelines contained

---

[48] *Scînteia*, July 9, 1957.

[49] An interesting biographic account of Maurer's political career may be found in J. F. Brown, *The New Eastern Europe* (New York: Praeger, 1966), pp. 287–289.

[50] *Scînteia*, September 17, 1957.

in the celebrated "Declaration" issued by the Kremlin during the Hungarian Revolution in October 1956. They also toned down the warning against exaggeration of "national peculiarities" and the dangers of dogmatism and revisionism.[51]

Recent studies of the 1957 Moscow meeting, the Sino-Soviet conflict, and the Rumanian deviation have provided new insight into the nature and extent of the Rumanians' utilization of the lessons of the Moscow conference. Far from supporting the theory of close Russo-Rumanian cooperation in the spirit of the Moscow Declaration and the basis of common interests, these and other materials reveal an intensification of Rumanian efforts to exploit the differences between China and Russia and the contradictions inherent in Khrushchev's plans for coexistence for their own benefit.[52] The first tangible result was the withdrawal of Russian troops from Rumania.

The Russian step was not, as heretofore assumed, a reflection of Khrushchev's confidence in Gheorghiu-Dej.[53] Nor was it prompted merely by his desire to impress the Western and noncommitted nations with his devotion to peaceful coexistence. The determining factor was instead a combination of Rumanian pressure exerted in conjunction with the Sino-Soviet controversy over the role of national armies in the nuclear age and Chinese support of the Rumanian position. The Rumanian argument for withdrawal was publicly stated on the occasion of an unheralded but highly significant trip by Stoica, Bodnăraş, and the Minister of Foreign Affairs, Avram Bunaciu, to the Middle and Far East in March 1958. First in Hanoi and subsequently in Peking, the Rumanians contrasted China's theory of reliance on national armies and corollary decision to withdraw its volunteers from North Korea with the American refusal to emulate the Chinese example. They also pointed out the incompatibility between peaceful coexistence and the maintenance of troops abroad.[54] While it may be argued that these views were

51 Gheorghiu-Dej, *Articole şi cuvîntări*, pp. 332–349.

52 Brown, *The New Eastern Europe*, pp. 202–211; Stephen Fischer-Galati, "Rumania: A Dissenting Voice in the Balkans," in Andrew Gyorgy, ed., *Issues of World Communism* (Princeton: Van Nostrand, 1966), pp. 127–142.

53 Ionescu, *Communism in Rumania*, pp. 288–291, provides the standard interpretation ignoring evidence brought out by students of the Sino-Soviet conflict. A review of East European problems in the context of the Sino-Soviet confrontation, with ample bibliographic references, is contained in William E. Griffith, ed., *Communism in Europe*, Vol. 2 (Cambridge, Mass.: The M.I.T. Press, 1966), pp. 8–13.

54 *Scînteia*, March 30 and April 9, 1958.

not too remote from Khrushchev's and thus that the withdrawal of the Soviet armies from Rumania was based on similar Russian considerations, it is noteworthy that the joint Sino-Rumanian communiqué, issued at the end of the Rumanians' visit, expressed positions clearly at variance with the Russians'. Most striking was the favorable comparison between Rumanian and Chinese Stalinist views on party discipline and ideological purity, the Chinese support of Rumanian diplomatic initiatives as a member of a socialist camp of equals, the reassertion of the need for strict observance of the principles governing relations of the "new type," and recognition of the Rumanian party's claims concerning its historic role of "social" and "national" liberator of the Rumanian people.[55] From what is known of the proceedings of the Warsaw Pact meeting of May 1958 such arguments could hardly have strengthened Khrushchev's confidence in the Chinese and Rumanians, and their reiteration apparently forced either the Russians' reluctant endorsement of the joint Sino-Rumanian request for withdrawal or "generous" acceptance of their advice.[56]

Stoica's, Bodnăraş's, and Bunaciu's trip itself was an assertion of Rumanian political individualism, albeit under the umbrella of Russia's nuclear power and leadership in Communist affairs. For apart from the strategic advantages to be derived from the "strengthening of fraternal ties" with China, the Rumanians also sought to reduce their economic dependence on Russia and the satellites by finding customers and markets in Communist and noncommitted Asian nations.[57] That this was at least one of the reasons for their safari is substantiated by their comparable and parallel moves in Western Europe and toward the United States, also possible under the all-embracing cover of peaceful coexistence. The relationship between these actions and the Rumanians' opposition to CMEA plans and policies has been shown by Professor Montias.[58] Rumania's nonconformist policies toward Yugoslavia must also be

---

[55] *Ibid.*, April 9, 1958.

[56] The Rumanian statements should be read in juxtaposition to the "Declaration of the States Participating at the Meeting of the Warsaw Treaty," *Pravda*, May 27, 1958.

[57] "Declaration of the President of the Council of Ministers of the Rumanian People's Republic and the Prime Minister of India," *Scînteia*, March 11, 1958; "Common Declaration of the President of the Council of Ministers of the Rumanian People's Republic and the Prime Minister of Burma," *ibid.*, April 2, 1958.

[58] See the forthcoming volume by John Michael Montias, *The Economic Development of Rumania* (Cambridge, Mass.: The M.I.T. Press, 1967).

understood in terms of the careful drive for self-assertion and "de-satellization."[59] While paying lip service to the general denuncia-tion of "revisionism," Bucharest maintained close relations with Belgrade throughout 1958. The policies—later described as Maurer's but whose underlying principles were apparently accepted in 1957 —were thus energetically pursued, in their embryonic form, in the months antedating the Plenum of November 1958. Even if the initial results were unspectacular, except for the withdrawal of the Soviet troops, the policies themselves became an integral part of Rumania's plans for socialist transformation *à la* Gheorghiu-Dej.

Gheorghiu-Dej's determination fully to control the process of socialist construction according to his interpretation of the "specific Rumanian conditions" also accounts for the policies of purification of Rumanian communism and society at large initiated in July 1957. Superficially the reign of terror directed against intellectuals, economic saboteurs, and revisionists of all kinds was in conformity with Khrushchev's own opposition to "revisionism" and anti-Lenin-ist practices in general. But actually the Rumanian actions were designed to secure total commitment, within and without the party, for the unflinching execution of Gheorghiu-Dej's essentially anti-Russian plans. It is noteworthy, however, that the terror, whose scope ranged from assaults against pro-Constantinescu "revision-ists" in the party to massive persecution of "revisionists" and eco-nomic malefactors in general, gained momentum in the summer of 1958 following the execution of Imre Nagy and the corollary *de facto* endorsement by Khrushchev of Gheorghiu-Dej's repressive measures. Thus under Russia's protective Stalinist umbrella, tem-porary as it was, Gheorghiu-Dej was able to purge all actual or potential opponents in the party, cow the population into total submission, and thus streamline the process of socialist construc-tion.[60] By November 1958, having reduced direct Soviet pressure through the Red Army and indirect pressure through party "lib-erals," having built as yet precarious bridges with nations other than members of CMEA and reinforced existing ones with China

59 Deviations from the Soviet line are apparent in the lengthy article "Cu privire la proiectul de program al Uniunii Communistilor din Iugoslavia" [Con-cerning the Draft Program of the Union of Communists in Yugoslavia], *Scînteia*, May 18, 19, 1958.

60 A good summary of the principal measures of oppression enacted and carried out in this period is contained in Ionescu, *Communism in Rumania*, pp. 289–291. The draconic resolution on party discipline adopted by the Plenum of the Central Committee of June 9–13, 1958 may be found in *Scînteia*, June 27, 1958.

and other members of the socialist camp, Gheorghiu-Dej and his closest associates, Stoica, Bodnăraş, Ceauşescu, and Maurer, were ready to make major and irrevocable plans for Rumania's future development.

The formal commitment to the socialist transformation of Rumania at all costs—but without great risk—was, in effect, made at the Plenum of November 1958. It is noteworthy that the rationale for the Rumanians' decision to accelerate the development of industry and agriculture was formally provided by Khrushchev's theories on the contribution of individual socialist states to the strength of the socialist camp as a whole and of their "simultaneous entrance into communism" rather than by the edicts of the Second Party Congress. This tactical maneuver reflected the Rumanians' awareness of the advantages that could be derived from endorsement of the Russian stance on simultaneous entry into communism but did not alter their determination to pursue their own plans for socialist construction, "desatellization," and diversification of external contacts. In fact, between November 1958 and the time when their plans met with overt Russian resistance, the Rumanians pursued a policy of getting all that the traffic would bear from Moscow while concurrently intensifying their search for economic and political alternatives.[61] And since the explicit commitment to economic development made in November 1958 and renewed during the Third Congress of the party in June 1960 ran counter to Russian interests, Rumania's political differences with Moscow gradually acquired an economic context. The acceptance of Khrushchev's economic and political views, as formally enunciated at the Russian party's Twenty-First Congress in January 1959, and the ensuing period of apparent harmony in Russo-Rumanian relations were facilitated by the superficial compatibility between the Russian and Rumanian blueprints for the future of the camp and the role of individual members. Nevertheless, even during the period of outward harmony, which was severely jolted in 1960 and came to a virtual end by 1961, deviations from Khrushchev's line and Russian tutelage were strikingly evident.

Foremost was the crystallization of "domesticism": increasing emphasis on the historic role of the party as the executor of both the "national" and "social" desiderata of the Rumanian people. The primacy of the Rumanian party and of the goal of national

[61] See footnote 47.

development, albeit in the context of the ultimate strength and victory of the socialist camp, became a popular argument from as early as February 1959. At that time, while still invoking the lessons of the Russian Twenty-First Congress and their validity in terms of each country's specific conditions, Gheorghiu-Dej asked for the Rumanians' total support for the execution of the party's program in terms of love and devotion to their fatherland and the Rumanian Workers' Party, "the continuator of the most glorious fighting traditions of the Rumanian people for its national and social liberation."[62] That the Russians were less than enthusiastic about this interpretation of Khrushchev's message and of their role in the shaping of Communist Rumania became evident by August 1959. They pointedly refrained from sending a high-level delegation to Bucharest on the occasion of the fifteenth anniversary of Rumania's liberation. Instead they dispatched Marshal Konev, symbolically chosen to stress Russia's military role in August 1944. During that month it also became known that the Kremlin had failed to satisfy Rumania's economic expectations. Gheorghiu-Dej's major address on August 23 confirmed that all was not well between Moscow and Bucharest and that the Rumanians were going to abide by their interpretation of the messages of the Twentieth and Twenty-First Congresses. The detailed reaffirmation of the party's paramount role in the country's national and social liberation since August 1944 and the justification of current policies in terms of the Rumanian plans first drawn in 1945, as revised in 1955, made the routine acceptance of Russian formulas on contemporary development of the socialist camp, Russia's leadership of the Communist movement, and relations between socialist and capitalist countries less convincing. Nor did the Russians ignore Gheorghiu-Dej's boasting over the rapid expansion of Rumania's economic and political relations with the West and noncommitted nations. In fact, Gheorghiu-Dej's statements promising the relentless pursuit of such policies as might be necessary to attain the party's goals and programs were largely designed to convince the Russians of the validity of the Rumanian positions. As these were at least theoretically compatible with the Russians' in all respects but the degree of subservience expected of the Rumanians, Gheorghiu-Dej in effect promised continuing allegiance to Moscow in return for Russian recognition of the Rumanians' policies and fulfillment of their economic needs.[63]

62 Gheorghiu-Dej's speech at the "Second National Conference of the Union of Student Associations in the Rumanian People's Republic" on February 19, 1959, *Scînteia*, February 20, 1959.

63 Gheorghiu-Dej's address, *ibid.*, August 23, 1959.

The Russians' lukewarm response to the Rumanians' pleas has been pointed out by students of Soviet-Rumanian economic relations. Without recapitulating the actions, discussions, and negotiations in this field—accounted for in Professor Montias' studies—it is evident that the differences had not been resolved by the time of the Rumanian party's Third Congress, and that this impasse determined the adoption of less veiled anti-Russian steps. However, even before the congress, the political bases were laid for strengthening Rumania's bargaining position with Moscow.

The exhortations for national support of the party's plans were accompanied throughout 1959 and early 1960 by economic and political concessions to the population. Increments in salaries and pensions, price reductions, relaxation of terror, and extension of the olive branch to "honest intellectuals" were all represented in terms of the party's interest in the people's well-being and as tangible evidence of the blessings of Rumanian socialism. Pragmatically, however, they were intended to secure mass support for an irrevocable economic commitment if not yet for a possible showdown with Moscow. Simultaneously, exploiting Khrushchev's commitment to peaceful coexistence, the regime speeded up its own mending of fences and, whenever feasible, building of economic bridges with the West. It also continued to pursue policies toward Yugoslavia and China which were at variance with those of Russia and her more faithful satellites.[64]

The Rumanian attacks on revisionism and condemnation of left-wing dogmatism were the most moderate in the bloc, reflecting specific national interests. In the case of Yugoslavia the Rumanians' primary concern was maintenance of correct interstate relationships; denunciation of revisionism on ideological grounds was not to prevent the promotion of projects of common interest, most notably the Stoica Plan. The extensive press coverage accorded to the celebration of the sixteenth anniversary of the proclamation of the Yugoslav Republic in November 1959 and the accompanying editorial comments applauding Yugoslav-Rumanian friendship, however, transcended the scope of a good-neighbor policy and of Russia's views on relations among socialist nations.[65] In fact, it was intended as an assertion of Gheorghiu-Dej's own positions on the rights of individual socialist nations to determine their political destinies in accordance with national peculiarities. The subsequent reiteration of the views expressed in November was also indicative of the Ru-

[64] A good summary discussion may be found in Ionescu, *Communism in Rumania*, pp. 288–315.
[65] *Scinteia*, November 29, 1959.

manians' determination to pursue Rumanian policies according to their interpretation of the Moscow Declaration and the Twenty-First Congress. This "independence" was manifest also in contemporary relations with China.

Whereas it would be difficult to demonstrate that policies toward China in 1959 and early 1960 were based on a complete realization of the growing differences between Moscow and Peking, it is clear that the Rumanians were aware of the Communist giants' conflicting interests and the possibility of exploiting these for their own benefit. The speech delivered by Defense Minister P'eng Teh-huai during an official visit to Bucharest in May 1959 exposed the ideological differences between China and Russia. The Rumanians' concurrent reiteration of their own interpretation of the Moscow Declaration of 1957, close as it was to the Russian, did not, however, totally reject the Chinese views. A common Sino-Rumanian bond could be found in the implicit and explicit statements by Maurer regarding relations among members of the socialist camp and of the worthiness of emulation of the Chinese policies of socialist construction.[66] The same themes were repeated in October 1959 on the occasion of the tenth anniversary of the Chinese People's Republic with even stronger emphasis placed on the Chinese achievements in domestic socialist construction and the strengthening of Rumanian-Chinese ties between 1952 and 1959.[67] The Rumanians' failure to endorse those elements of the Chinese line which were in contradiction with their own, particularly with respect to Yugoslavia and the West, in no way affected the cordiality of the relations between the two nations and parties. From the Rumanian point of view, endorsed by the Chinese, China's contribution to the unity of the socialist camp and the strengthening of individual member nations was invaluable.

The exacerbation of the Sino-Soviet dispute on the occasion of the Warsaw Pact meeting of February 1960 and publication of China's anti-Russian ideological tirade "Long Live Leninism!" in April could not have gone unnoticed in Bucharest. The demotion of Russia to the position of a senior member but not leader of the socialist camp by Gheorghiu-Dej in March 1960 and the restatement of this formula in following months cannot be connected directly to *refroidissement* in Sino-Soviet relations.[68] But it represented an

66 *Ibid.*, May 23, 1959.
67 *Ibid.*, October 1, 1959.
68 Gheorghiu-Dej's speech at the regional party conference in Cluj on March 13, 1960, *ibid.*, March 17, 1960.

assertion of Rumania's own interpretation of intercamp relations subsequent to the Warsaw Pact meeting. Nevertheless, it may be more than a coincidence that the outlining, in March, of the themes to be stressed at the Third Congress was concurrent with the abandonment of the concept of Russian leadership of a camp of equals and that this position duplicated the Chinese views. Moreover, the reiteration, at the same time, of the correctness of the party's foreign policies toward China, Yugoslavia, the West, and the Soviet Union, and of its domestic course—all Rumanian—reflected a degree of strength and security that was at least partly derived from evaluation of the "objective factors" underlying Russia's and Rumania's relations with the rest of the world if not necessarily with each other.[69] Since perhaps the primary objective of the Third Party Congress, formally convoked only late in April, was the establishment of Russo-Rumanian relations on a more realistic basis, the Rumanians' case for recognition and support of their attainments and goals by the Soviet Union was obviously strengthened by any and all factors that would weaken the Russians' means for exerting pressures detrimental to Rumania's interests. Among these factors the Chinese deviation was not to be minimized. The Sino-Soviet confrontation at the Rumanian party's congress in June was not totally unexpected by Gheorghiu-Dej. When it occurred, it provided the Rumanians with a trump card in addition to those of party strength and unity, diversification of Rumania's economic bases, national support for socialist construction *à la roumaine* which Gheorghiu-Dej so skillfully exposed in his game with Moscow. The process of consolidation of his power and establishment of the foundations for socialist construction according to his prescriptions, begun in 1952, was sufficiently complete to permit presentation of a long-range plan for Rumania's socialist development in June 1960. The overcoming of Russian resistance, the ever-present obstacle to the attainment of Gheorghiu-Dej's plans, was doubtlessly facilitated by changing domestic and international conditions. The Third Party Congress was to record these changes and to provide the blueprint for the attainment of the party's historic goals within a shorter period than expected even by Gheorghiu-Dej and his associates.

[69] Gheorghiu-Dej's speeches immediately antedating the Third Party Congress may be found in Gheorghe Gheorghiu-Dej, *Artikel und Reden, August 1959–Mai 1961* [Articles and Speeches, August 1959–May 1961] (Bucharest: Politischer Verlag, 1961), pp. 68–107.

CHAPTER FOUR

THE ROAD TO INDEPENDENCE (1960–1964)

The lengthy and formal report of the Central Committee of the Rumanian Workers' Party submitted by Gheorghiu-Dej to the Third Congress was anything but a rehashing of worn-out clichés and a list of unrealizable plans and promises.[1] By virtue of hindsight it is possible to point out that the implementation of his recommendations, accepted by the congress, would inevitably have led to a deepening of the cleavage between Rumania and Russia and furtherance of the "independent" Rumanian course which became a reality three years later. But even the casual student of Rumanian and international communism should have realized at the end of the Third Congress that Gheorghiu-Dej's report, the resolutions of the assembly, and its communiqué recorded the inalterable fact that irreversible changes had occurred in Rumania and the international Communist community since the Second Congress of 1955 and that the Rumanians were ready to exploit the new conditions for their own benefit.

The extremely ambitious program for economic development for 1960–1965 and the goals of the projected Fifteen-Year Plan must have given pause to the Russians.[2] As described by John Michael Montias, the Rumanians' unilateral commitment of Russia to the extension of credits and technical assistance beyond and even contrary to Khrushchev's own plans for Rumania's economic role in the socialist camp did not augur well for the future of Soviet-Rumanian relations.[3] The alternative of greater Rumanian dependence on Western support was also less than palatable to Moscow. The Rumanians' determination to pursue their goal of rapid multilateral industrialization and socialization of agriculture, repeatedly

1 Gheorghe Gheorghiu-Dej, *Raport la cel de al III-lea congres al Partidului Muncitoresc Romîn* [Report of the Rumanian Workers' Party at the Third Party Congress] (Bucharest: Editura Politică, 1960), pp. 5–126.

2 *Ibid.*, pp. 19–85.

3 John Michael Montias' forthcoming book, *The Economic Development of Rumania* (Cambridge, Mass.: The M.I.T. Press, 1967).

underlined during the proceedings of the Third Congress, was, however, unmistakable. It was reflected in specific political changes recorded at the time. The very composition of the party and its leadership revealed unprecedented cohesion and unity of purpose. Gheorghiu-Dej's team was in complete command of the Politburo, Secretariat, and Central Committee. Gheorghiu-Dej, Chivu Stoica, Apostol, Bodnăraş, Ceauşescu, Drăghici, and Moghioroş were joined by Maurer and constituted the hard core of the industrial- and national-oriented Politburo. The Central Committee was significantly enlarged from 92 to 110 full and candidate-members. It included an unusually large number of technocrats and professional and intellectual cadres dedicated to the attainment of Gheorghiu-Dej's goals. The party itself had grown from less than 600,000 members in 1955 to nearly 850,000, and the *aktiv* had reached 150,000. And even if the social composition was not up to the rulers' expectations and the cohesion alluded to by Gheorghiu-Dej in his report had not yet been attained at all levels, the preponderance of industrial workers, well-trained technocrats, managers, and professionals made the execution of the program adopted in 1960 more than probable.

The only fears expressed by the leadership during the Third Congress were related to possible internal and external subversion of its plans. The prevalence of "bourgeois" ideological influences and the absence of socialist discipline among the youth and population at large were duly recorded and the proper Stalinist corrective measures recommended. But this apprehension, though more forcefully expressed, was less serious than the Rumanians' concern over the repercussions of the growing Sino-Soviet conflict in the socialist camp and the international community in general. If any doubts of a rift between China and Russia existed prior to the Bucharest meeting, they were dispelled at that time.[4] Ideologically, the Rumanian position was closer to the Russian than the Chinese, but the Rumanians were unprepared to take sides for fear that a total commitment to Russia would strengthen the country's dependence on Moscow. But even without such commitment the Rumanians feared that the conflict could lead to the polarization of the socialist camp, with nefarious consequences for members of the Soviet bloc seeking *de facto* "desatellization." The Rumanian posi-

4 See particularly G. F. Hudson, Richard Lowenthal, and Roderick MacFarquhar, *The Sino-Soviet Dispute* (New York: Praeger, 1961), pp. 132–141, and Edward Crankshaw, *The New Cold War, Moscow vs. Pekin* (Harmondsworth, England: Penguin, 1963), pp. 97–110.

tion, explicitly enunciated after the issuance of the Bucharest Communiqué and restated following the celebrated Moscow Conference of December, was to support the essential Russian arguments on peaceful coexistence and ultimate victory of socialism over capitalism but hedge on the Russian prescription for the attainment of unity in the socialist camp.[5] The Rumanian formula, adopting the Chinese views on equality of all members of the socialist community, envisaged the attainment of that unity and the subsequent triumph of socialism through the contributions of all member nations to the common cause. According to Gheorghiu-Dej, the roads to the ultimate victory of socialism varied according to specific national conditions and were all correct as long as charted by orthodox interpreters of Marxism-Leninism. In Rumania's case the party had indicated the correct path since 1945. The decisions of the Third Congress merely advanced the process of socialist transformation to enable Rumania to make the maximum contribution to the strength and ultimate victory of communism. The attainment of that supreme goal did not preclude collaboration with capitalist or nonsocialist nations; in fact, such was to be encouraged as contributory to the cause of peace and peaceful competition among opposing socioeconomic and political systems. Stripped of dialectical verbalism, the Rumanian message was clear. Gheorghiu-Dej and his associates were, in effect, demanding optimum Russian economic assistance for the attainment of the goals of the Third Congress and noninterference in Rumania's internal and foreign affairs in return for Rumanian support of Russia's positions in international matters. It is clear that the Rumanians did not expect unconditional Russian acceptance of their theses and demands. But it must have been encouraging to them that the protracted economic negotiations conducted by Bîrlădeanu and his associates during the spring of 1960 and formalized only in November after the violent Sino-Soviet confrontation in Bucharest reflected a growing Russian concern for satisfying the demands of individual members of the bloc.[6] However, even if possibilities for gaining concessions from Moscow appeared to have increased after the Bucharest meeting, the Rumanians, with characteristic lack of confidence in the Kremlin and true to their own policy of diversification, pursued their drive to obtain alternate means of economic

---

5 Speeches by Gheorghiu-Dej on June 25, 1960, August 30, 1960, December 19-20, 1960, *Scînteia*, June 26, August 31, and December 22, 1960.

6 On these points see J. F. Brown, "Rumania Steps Out of Line," *Survey*, No. 49 (October 1963), pp. 21-22.

assistance from the West. The specter of specialization and integration of the economies of the bloc under CMEA was clearly a factor in this *rapprochement* with the capitalists. Moreover, the Russians were still reluctant as well as unable to provide the Rumanians with the wherewithal, whereas the West seemed ready to build political bridges to the satellites on the basis of "relations of the new type." The settlement of outstanding economic problems with the United States, England, and Denmark and the conclusion of meaningful trade agreements with non-Communist countries provided potential leverage on Russia over and above that available through maintenance of friendly interstate relations with "heretics" in the socialist camp. It is indeed noteworthy that despite the condemnation of "Yugoslav revisionism" and "left-wing dogmatism" (presumably Chinese) the Rumanians concluded a long-term economic agreement with Yugoslavia in December 1960 and applauded the Chinese achievements in the construction of socialism on the occasion of the eleventh anniversary of the proclamation of the Chinese People's Republic.[7]

It is probable that the Rumanians would have pursued their objectives with greater vigor after the Moscow Conference had it not been for the worsening of the international situation over Berlin and the temporary lull in the Sino-Soviet dispute. But these external circumstances that dominated the better part of 1961 did not wholly arrest the execution of the plans adopted in 1960. Ostensibly the Rumanians were concentrating on socialist construction at home in close coordination with members of the socialist camp and the Soviet Union. In actuality, however, they continued to dig the ground from under the CMEA and to exploit Khrushchev's need for a united bloc in anticipation of possible confrontations with the West and China.[8] These policies were bound to have repercussions both at home and abroad; Gheorghiu-Dej and his associates therefore began preparations for all contingencies.

In Rumania proper the leadership initiated the first moves toward meaningful social and national reconciliation since 1956–

[7] A review of these policies is contained in the editorial devoted to the Moscow Declaration of December 1960, "Sub steagul invincibil al Marxism-Leninismului" [Under the Invincible Banner of Marxism-Leninism], *Scînteia*, December 7, 1960, and, in greater detail, in Gheorghiu-Dej's address to a Central Committee plenum on December 19–20, 1960, *ibid.*, December 22, 1960.

[8] A brief but intelligent analysis of Rumanian policies is contained in David Floyd, *Rumania: Russia's Dissident Ally* (New York: Praeger, 1965), pp. 56–69, hereafter cited as Floyd, *Rumania*.

1957. Despite the frequent advocacy of the theory that the class struggle had to continue during the new era of "peaceful coexistence"—clearly intended to dispel Rumanian expectations that the economic *rapprochement* with the West would result in "liberalization" at home—the regime did, in fact, seek a *rapprochement* with all Rumanians. The unifying factor was to be socialist patriotism. Through its acceptance, as a substitute for bourgeois nationalism, the class struggle would be resolved. This was the message conveyed to the Rumanian people by the party leadership during the electoral campaign of February and March 1961. The elections to the Grand National Assembly were to constitute a vote of popular confidence and support of the policies of the party as formulated at the Third Congress. The endless recapitulation of the party's historic interest in the people's well-being was accompanied by sentimental appeals to the Rumanians' love of country and by patriotic slogans unprecedented in Communist electoral campaigns.[9] The tone of the speeches and manifestos was not accidental. It was calculated to impress the Russians and the members of the bloc with the "granitelike" determination of the leadership and the Rumanian people to complete socialist construction according to Gheorghiu-Dej's blueprint. The reorganization of the structure of the principal state organs by the Grand National Assembly elected in March was also indicative of that determination. Gheorghiu-Dej's concurrent assumption of the dual role of First Secretary of the party and President of the newly created State Council was less significant than the replacement of Chivu Stoica by Ion Gheorghe Maurer as Prime Minister. To the initiated, Maurer represented disengagement from Russia and further *rapprochement* with the West as well as domestic "liberalization." Stoica, a mediocre party functionary, was no longer adequate as leader of a government intent on strengthening relations with the non-Communist world and sporting a "new look." The quest for respectability and acceptance of Rumanian communism at home and abroad reached greater proportions after March 1961.

It has been indicated by serious students of Soviet-Rumanian economic relations and of the CMEA that the essential irreconcilability between the Rumanian and the Russian, East German, and

---

9 See, for instance, the "Manifesto of the Central Council of the People's Democratic Front," *Scînteia*, February 16, 1961; editorial "Pentru înflorirea patriei socialiste, pentru pace și bună stare" [For the Blossoming of the Socialist Fatherland, for Peace and Prosperity], *ibid.*, February 17, 1961; and Gheorghiu-Dej's main electoral speech, *ibid.*, March 4, 1961.

Czechoslovak views on national specialization in the bloc became evident after March 1961.[10] If a showdown was averted for a relatively long time, it was because of the Russians' unwillingness to provoke a crisis in the bloc on the eve of a possible confrontation with the West over Berlin, and the Rumanians' reluctance to force the issue under inauspicious international conditions, rather than because of alteration of Bucharest's basic positions. But it is noteworthy that in the aftermath of the "Bay of Pigs" episode and the Kennedy-Khrushchev Vienna meeting, the Rumanians sent a high-powered delegation headed by Moghioroş to the United States, allegedly for the study of agricultural techniques but actually to investigate possibilities for American economic assistance. Concurrently, a far-reaching, long-range economic agreement was concluded with Italy.[11]

Whereas these weapons were insufficient per se to sway Moscow into accepting the Rumanian plans for industrialization, they could be used in conjunction with reserve power derived from Khrushchev's dilemmas of the summer of 1961. It is now known that the Rumanians reacted unfavorably to the grand plan for military and economic integration à la russe presented in Moscow to members of the Warsaw Pact and CMEA on August 3–5 and spelled out in greater detail during the immediately following bilateral Soviet-Rumanian discussions. The formidable Rumanian delegation, including Gheorghiu-Dej, Maurer, Ceauşescu, and Bîrlădeanu, was apparently unable to persuade the Russians and their supporters of the necessity to adapt themselves to the Rumanian views on integration, and the matter was left in abeyance pending further multilateral and bilateral pourparlers among members of the bloc.[12] It is also known that the Rumanians engaged in a holding operation after their return to Bucharest, awaiting the development of a more favorable international climate for pursuit of their own schemes. Whether they expected Khrushchev to make a frontal attack on the Albanians and Chinese at the Twenty-Second CPSU Congress, whose essential features were outlined to the members of the Warsaw Pact in August, is unknown. It has been initimated recently that Gheorghiu-Dej did, in fact, stall the Russians' plans

10 See Montias, *The Economic Development of Rumania* and Brown, "Rumania," *op. cit.*, pp. 22–26.

11 The tactical implications of these steps become evident from a careful reading of Gheorghiu-Dej's report to the June 30–July 1 Central Committee Plenum on the execution of the directives of the Third Congress (*Scînteia*, July 2, 1961).

12 The official communiqué, without commentary, is in *Scînteia*, August 13, 1961.

for rapid integration in 1961 by trading Rumanian support for Russia's position vis-à-vis Albania and China for Moscow's limited endorsement of the Rumanian objectives and course. This interpretation is at least partly substantiated by the Rumanian communiqué issued at the end of the Moscow meeting and by Gheorghiu-Dej's report on that meeting and speech on August 23—all condemning left-wing dogmatism—and the formal, yet restrained, condemnation of the Albanian and Chinese heresies at the CPSU Congress in October.[13] What is known, however, is that the Rumanians were greatly relieved by the peaceful settlement of the Berlin crisis and the subsequent possibilities for further normalization of relations with the West. Gheorghiu-Dej's speech of August 23 laid unusually strong emphasis on Rumania's desire for improved relations with the West, her devotion to peaceful coexistence, and the correlation between the mandate of the Third Congress and the desiderata mentioned earlier.[14] Nor was it by accident that the regime saw fit concurrently to intensify its campaign to win over the Rumanian people to its cause by holding out the rosiest prospects to the builders of a prosperous socialist fatherland and even by seeking accommodation with the most inveterate class enemy, the political prisoners of long standing. Whether these domestic moves were made primarily to facilitate the expansion of relations with the West or to strengthen internal cohesion in anticipation of the far-reaching decisions that were to be adopted by the CPSU Twenty-Second Congress is not entirely clear. In any event, they could be justified in terms of the policy of national reconciliation and unification as well as the pursuit of the course enacted by the Third Congress.

The CPSU Twenty-Second Congress actually precipitated the crystallization of this Rumanian course. The impact on Rumania of Khrushchev's statements and the resolutions of the congress was much more profound in the area of Soviet-Rumanian economic relations than that of internal de-Stalinization. The vigorous denunciation of Stalin, the cult of personality, and the related excommunication of the Albanian leadership (and by implication the Chinese) was taken in stride by Gheorghiu-Dej. But the consequences that polarization of the socialist camp would have on the execution of Rumania's plans for economic development accentuated the very fears that the Rumanians had entertained since 1960.

13 Compare Gheorghiu-Dej's speeches of August and October, in *ibid.*, August 23, October 21, 1961, respectively.
14 *Ibid.*, August 23, 1961.

To fend off the Russian octopus, which could be kept at bay in the area of de-Stalinization now that all genuine anti-Stalinists had been purged, the Rumanian leadership concentrated on the containment of Khrushchev's plans for economic integration under the CMEA. The Rumanians' method was to cling stubbornly to their traditional interpretation of the role of the party in the construction of socialism and to differentiate between Gheorghiu-Dejism and Russianism in general. After October 1961 the Rumanians' denunciation of Stalinism was direct; that of Khrushchevism was, however, implied in their interpretation of the message of the Twenty-Second Congress. The various official pronunciamentos left no doubt that in the view of the Rumanian leadership the party alone had always been the best judge of what was necessary for the attainment of the national goal and that certain measures had not been adopted earlier because of external interference in Rumanian internal affairs.[15] According to this doctrine, the process of socialist construction was hampered by Stalin's agents in Rumania and their successors—Pauker, Luca, Constantinescu, and Chişinevski—as well as by other internal and external forces seeking to impede the realization of the party's historic program. Khrushchev and his supporters were not specifically excluded from membership in or complicity with these hostile forces, loosely identified as "imperialists," "revisionists," "dogmatists," and exponents of "bourgeois ideology." In fact, Rumanian statements and actions between October 1961 and the first open collision with Khrushchev in June 1962 revealed the party's suspicion of Khrushchevism as much as they did its determination to consolidate its national and international bases for a possible showdown with Moscow. Even if the Rumanians did not seek to embark upon a collision course with the Kremlin, they did not necessarily avoid it. If prudence prevailed between October 1961 and June 1962, it was on the expectation that Moscow would agree to a compromise formula that would be consistent with the Rumanian desiderata. But when the relatively subtle methods of "persuasion" failed in the summer of 1962, the Rumanians had consolidated their position sufficiently to risk escalation of the dispute even to the point of no return.[16]

The crude attempts to exonerate Gheorghiu-Dej of Stalinism and

15 By far the most important statement is Gheorghiu-Dej's report on the Twenty-Second Congress presented to the November 30–December 5 Central Committee Plenum, *ibid.*, December 7, 1961.

16 Consult Gheorghiu-Dej's speeches made between December 1961 and June 1962 in Gheorghe Gheorghiu-Dej, *Artikel und Reden, Juni 1961–Dezember 1962* [Articles and Speeches, June 1961–December 1962] (Bucharest: Politischer Verlag, 1963), pp. 206–447.

to ascribe all the "crimes" condemned by Khrushchev in October 1961 to Ana Pauker, Vasile Luca, Miron Constantinescu, and Iosif Chişinevski so flabbergasted all but the initiated that Gheorghiu-Dej's true intentions were generally unnoticed. The repetition of these allegations and the slow tempo of de-Stalinization reconfirmed to critics of the regime the validity of the then prevalent stereotypes characterizing the "crude" Rumanian leadership. Moreover, the Rumanians' denunciation of Albanian heresies and support of the Russian principles on international relations were interpreted as evidence of unflagging Rumanian loyalty to Moscow and of unconditional adherence to the Soviet line in all matters other than de-Stalinization. Certain unheralded moves, ultimately of greater significance, then received but scanty consideration.

The "red thread" in all Rumanian interpretations of the message of the Twenty-Second Congress was the congress' condemnation of the Stalinist principle and practice of interference in other countries' internal affairs. The view that the Soviet congress in fact endorsed Gheorghiu-Dejism was expressed methodically throughout Rumania by the top echelons of the party in January when urgent demands were made to speed up the process of industrialization and agricultural collectivization.[17] This official interpretation, with strong nationalist and anti-Russian overtones, was understood by the "leading cadres" and the intellectual community at large. And it was to prevent this "nationalist appreciation" from assuming a dangerously anti-Russian character that Gheorghiu-Dej personally carried the party's message of moderation to the now celebrated Writers' Conference in January 1962.[18] This intervention, unlike that of 1957, sought to define the limits of coexistence between "bourgeois chauvinism" and "socialist patriotism" rather than to condemn "nationalist" trends in literature and the arts per se. The writers were asked, and they agreed, to sing the praises of the party as the architect, and the people as the constructors, of a great socialist Rumanian fatherland. They were, however, to desist from raising, or succumbing to, "bourgeois nationalist" passions still prevalent among "certain circles," which could only be equated with the population at large and its latent anti-Russian sentiments. But these admonitions for caution did not alter the leadership's ultimate intent to strengthen its ties with the intellectual community and the population in general in order to obtain the common Rumanian national goal. In April, following the announcement of

17 *Scînteia*, January 1962, *passim*.
18 *Ibid.*, January 25, 1962.

the completion of collectivization, a Central Committee plenum took special pains to hail this achievement in the now customary terms of the correctness of the party's policies and dedication of the Rumanians to the construction of a new fatherland.[19] At the same plenum, the process of national reconciliation and mass identification with the leadership was dramatically extended through a revision of the criteria for admission to the Rumanian Workers' Party. The opening of the ranks of the party to former members of "the late bourgeois parties" and to all other Rumanians, "regardless of social position," who were dedicated to Gheorghiu-Dejism was at least as significant as the concurrent decision to increase the proportion of peasants in the organization.[20]

By themselves these moves had no more of an anti-Russian character than the consolidation of existing, and acceleration of the search for new, trade agreements with nations not belonging to CMEA. But they were designed to provide the Rumanians with sufficient ammunition to secure acceptance of their views on socialist economic integration by other members at the celebrated meeting of the Council held in Moscow in June 1962.

It has been generally recognized by students of the CMEA and of Soviet-Rumanian relations that the basically anti-Rumanian decisions adopted in Moscow and the Rumanian reaction to them constitute the formal beginning of the "independent course."[21] In brief, the Rumanians took exception to the principle of subordination of national to bloc interests which the Russians and their closest supporters, the Czechs and East Germans, were seeking to impose on their partners. If the Rumanian protest against the decisions reached in Moscow was somewhat restrained, it was only because the formulas incorporated in the final communiqué were sufficiently flexible and ambiguous to allow circumvention.[22] On paper at least, subordination of national to bloc interests did not expressly preclude the development of strong national economies. Moreover, the stated possibility of transforming the CMEA into a truly international organization permitted, even if only in theory,

[19] Ibid., April 26, 1962. See also Gheorghiu-Dej's report to an extraordinary session of the Grand National Assembly regarding completion of collectivization and related problems, ibid., April 28, 1962.

[20] Ibid., May 17, 1962.

[21] Brown, "Rumania," op. cit., pp. 19–34; Floyd, Rumania, pp. 70–99. The economic significance and general political consequences of the Moscow meeting are also discussed by Professor Montias in The Economic Development of Rumania.

[22] Text of the communiqué: Scînteia, June 9, 1962.

bilateral expansion of Rumania's economic relations with non-members of the bloc. Nevertheless, the Rumanians took great pains to emphasize in their initial commentary on the Moscow decisions those aspects of their interpretation of the communiqué which diverged from the Russians'.[23] Their insistence on the correctness of the resolutions of the Third Congress on economic and political affairs, on the requirement of "taking into account of specific national characteristics and possibilities" in formulating international policies, and on the right ultimately to determine what was best for Rumania and, by extension, the socialist camp amounted to a *de facto* rejection of principles advocated by Moscow.

Whether any compromise would have been possible between the Rumanian views on integration and specialization and those of the Soviet Union following the Moscow meeting remains a matter of conjecture. But it is clear that the prospects for reconciliation of the opposing positions were substantially reduced after Khrushchev's visit to Rumania during the second half of June and his refusal to satisfy the Rumanians' demands. The Russians declined to accept Gheorghiu-Dej's contention that the enormous economic progress attained by his country under the party's tested leadership was sufficient to justify further development of its heavy industry in a manner incompatible with the attainment of the CMEA's plans for international specialization and general economic integration of the bloc.[24] Gheorghiu-Dej's counterarguments, centering on earlier Russian commitments to Rumania and the party's to the multilateral development of the Rumanian economy, carried little weight with the Russians.[25] It is known that, oratorical courtesies aside, Khrushchev left Rumania, at the end of what was to be his last official visit to that country, determined to break Gheorghiu-Dej's resistance to Russia's plans for bloc integration. Gheorghiu-Dej's own determination to resist "external interference" in Rumanian affairs was, in turn, comparably strengthened. The collision was temporarily averted only because the international situation in the summer of 1962 was not conducive to unilateral removal of the barriers to Rumania's road to independence. But the Rumanian path was smoothed after the Cuban confrontation in the fall.

23 *Scînteia* editorial, "Sub steagul internaţionalismului!" [Under the Banner of Internationalism!], June 11, 1962.

24 Khrushchev's views are most clearly expressed in his parting speech, *ibid.*, June 25, 1962.

25 The Rumanian position was clearly stated in Gheorghiu-Dej's own statements, *ibid.*, June 25, 1962, and the editorial "Sub semnul prieteniei frăţesti" [Under the Sign of Fraternal Friendship], *ibid.*, June 28, 1962.

Shortly thereafter the Rumanians pushed their claims with unprecedented courage and vigor at the risk of a direct confrontation with the Kremlin and without regard for the integrity of the CMEA, the Soviet bloc, and the socialist camp as a whole. In fact, even before the first overt defiance of Russia which occurred late in November, the Rumanian leadership countered every attempt by Moscow to force her will upon Bucharest and underscored the validity of all Rumanian premises and policies.

Khrushchev's pronunciamento on "Essential Questions in the Development of the World Socialist System," in which he pressed his views on economic integration, implicitly criticized the Rumanians' "autarchic tendencies" and "trading on the side." But the veiled threat of economic sanctions against nonconformists failed to impress Gheorghiu-Dej.[26] In the same month of August 1962, Alexandru Drăghici, speaking for Gheorghiu-Dej, stated more explicitly than ever the party's role in shaping Rumania's destiny since it liberated the country in August 1944 and pledged the fulfillment of the goals traced at the Third Congress on the basis of existing plans.[27] In September, the Rumanians rebuffed Ulbricht's views on the CMEA, paralleling Khrushchev's, on the occasion of what has been widely regarded as a East German mission on Moscow's behalf. At that time, Gheorghiu-Dej personally repeated the Rumanian arguments justifying opposition to integration à la russe.[28] And it was also in September that Gheorghiu-Dej and Maurer undertook an extensive trip to India and Indonesia in search of closer economic ties and opportunities to impress the tiers monde with Rumania's growing power and prestige. The main themes stressed by the Rumanian leaders in their numerous speeches—Rumania's desire to expand trade relations with all nations and determination to attain the goals established by the Third Congress—were apparently as offensive to Moscow as the restatement of current views on the CMEA. Nor was Gheorghiu-Dej's comparison between Rumania and the host countries, as fellow nations united by the common bonds of "self-liberation" and makers of their own destinies, to Khrushchev's liking.[29] A trade agree-

26 *The Current Digest of the Soviet Press* (hereafter cited as *CDSP*), Vol. XIV, No. 36, October 3, 1962, pp. 3–4, contains a translation of Khrushchev's statement.
27 *Scînteia*, August 23, 1962.
28 *Ibid.*, September 16, 1962.
29 See particularly Gheorghiu-Dej's Indonesian speeches, *ibid.*, October 5 and 6, 1962.

ment whereby the Rumanians were to acquire from India the iron ore denied to them by Russia must have added to the Russians' displeasure. In any event, the Rumanian actions failed to persuade Khrushchev to alter his stand on Rumania's role in bloc economic planning and integration.

It is an open question whether the Russians would have taken more drastic steps than verbal exchanges to coerce the Rumanians into accepting their formula had it not been for the Cuban confrontation. But in the immediate aftermath of that crisis, which resulted in an exacerbation of the Sino-Soviet conflict and exposed the comparative Russian weakness vis-à-vis the United States, the Kremlin was unprepared to take any action that would further jeopardize the unity of the bloc and of the socialist camp in general. The Rumanians' immediate reaction to the Cuban crisis was to lend support to Khrushchev's policies on the condition that the Russians adopt a more conciliatory position toward the Rumanian views of the role and rights of individual members of the bloc, camp, and the CMEA. That this was the price of Rumanian support became evident in Gheorghiu-Dej's speech on the occasion of the forty-fifth anniversary of the October Revolution[30] and Gheorghe Apostol's at the Eighth Congress of the Communist Party of Bulgaria.[31] On November 7 and 8 respectively, these men reiterated the correctness of Rumanian policies of socialist construction, the need for socialist unity, and the disservice rendered that unity and the principles of the Moscow Declaration of 1960 by the Albanians and their supporters, the Chinese. It is known that high-level discussions among bloc leaders were held in Sofia and in Budapest on the occasion of the Eighth Congress of the Hungarian party, which met on the heels of the Bulgarian Assembly. While details of the conversations are unknown, it is clear that the Rumanian positions did not receive the endorsement of the Russians, East Germans, Czechs, and possibly other members of the bloc. To step up their pressure on Moscow and its supporters, the Rumanians convened, during the meeting of the Hungarian Eighth Congress, a special plenum of the Central Committee which made some startling decisions.[32]

It was certainly not by accident that on November 21, Alexandru Drăghici deleted from his address to the Hungarian Eighth Con-

---

30 *Ibid.*, November 8, 1962.
31 *Ibid.*, November 9, 1962.
32 See the official communiqué regarding the Plenum of November 21–23, 1962, *ibid.*, November 24, 1962.

gress all references to Albania and China while reiterating Rumania's determination to carry out the plans approved by the Third Congress.[33] Nor was it possible to interpret the communiqué issued by the plenum, stressing the correctness of Rumania's views on integration and publicizing the promotion of the country's delegate to the CMEA and chief exponent of the "autarchic" position, Alexandru Bîrlădeanu, to the post of alternate member of the Politburo as a gesture of friendship toward Moscow.[34] But the announcement on November 25 that an Anglo-French consortium would build the steel plant at Galați, the focal point of the Soviet-Rumanian dispute on industrialization, left no doubt as to the Rumanians' determination to develop heavy industry regardless of Soviet objections. Having faced the Russians with this *fait accompli,* Gheorghiu-Dej and his associates added insult to injury by approving two supplementary anti-Russian actions. On November 29 *Scînteia* published a lengthy editorial on "The Anniversary of Albania's Liberation" applauding the achievements of the Albanian party in the construction of socialism,[35] and in the December issue of the *Annals of the Historical Institute of the Central Committee of the Rumanian Workers' Party* a frontal attack was delivered against the traditional Russian interpretation of Rumania's liberation from fascism in August 1944.[36] Rumania's liberation now became the achievement of the Rumanian party and the Rumanian armed forces "assisted" by Soviet comrades in arms.

The Russian response to these actions appears to have been unsatisfactory to the Rumanians. Neither Ceaușescu's address to the Tenth Congress of the Italian Party[37] nor Bodnăraș' to the Twelfth Czech Congress,[38] nor the proposals submitted to the seventeenth session of the CMEA in Bucharest[39]—all occurring in December—

[33] *Ibid.,* November 22, 1962.

[34] *Ibid.,* November 24, 1962.

[35] *Ibid.,* November 29, 1962.

[36] Gheorghe Țuțui, "Poziția forțelor democrate față de monarhie în perioada 23 august 1944–30 decembrie 1947" [Position of the Democratic Forces toward the Monarchy during the Period August 23, 1944–December 30, 1947] *Analalele Institutului de Istorie a Partidului de pe lîngă C.C. al P.M.R.,* Vol. VIII, No. 6 (1962), pp. 44–70, restates in somewhat stronger and more explicit terms the arguments contained in a similar article by Vl. Zaharescu, "Istoria partidului și a legăturilor lui cu masele—factor hotărîtor pentru organizarea și înfăptuirea insurecției armate din august 1944" [History of the Party and Its Relations with the Masses—Decisive Factor in Organizing and Achieving the Armed Insurrection of August 1944], *ibid.,* Vol. VIII, No. 4 (1962), pp. 3–19.

[37] *Scînteia,* December 6, 1962.

[38] *Ibid.,* December 7, 1962.

[39] *Ibid.,* December 23, 1962.

resulted in acceptance of Bucharest's theories on industrialization and intrabloc relations in general. Under the circumstances, the Rumanians intensified their drive for recognition on the occasion of the fifteenth anniversary of the establishment of the Rumanian People's Republic on December 30. Gheorghiu-Dej, Maurer, and Apostol all repeated the current positions on the CMEA and related matters and made into official dogma the theory of Rumania's liberation by the Rumanian party and the Rumanian armed forces fighting side by side with the Soviet armies.[40] The Rumanians' statements themselves were blunt enough, but to Russia's discomfiture the Chinese endorsement of Rumanian views was even blunter. In a telegram that left little to the imagination Mao Tse-tung, Liu Shao-ch'i, Chu Teh, and Chou En-lai proclaimed the Rumanian party and the Rumanian people the sole liberators of their country and shapers of their socialist destiny and expressed full support for the Rumanians' determination to carry out their plans for socialist construction. The prominent publication of the Chinese message and of the Rumanian reply acknowledging its validity was obviously designed to strengthen Rumania's case against Moscow.[41]

In view of Rumanian actions subsequent to the anniversary, it is clear that in the total reappraisal of the international situation in general and socialist camp relations in particular made by the Rumanian leadership in November and December 1962, the Sino-Soviet conflict played a more decisive part than has heretofore been assumed. Gheorghiu-Dej and his associates reached two fundamental conclusions on the eve of 1963: that the Sino-Soviet conflict was irreversible and that the Soviet Union, despite its opposition to Rumanian policies, could not bring Gheorghiu-Dej to heel in the aftermath of the Cuban crisis. They therefore decided to pursue a strategy that would ensure if not Moscow's outright acceptance of Bucharest's views on the CMEA at least the unhindered pursuit of the independent course. It is known that the opposing Russian and Rumanian views on economic integration were not reconciled at the CMEA meeting held in Bucharest in December largely because of Rumanian intransigence. And Rumania's attitude remained unaltered by the time of the following meeting of the council in Moscow in February 1963. The unprecedented denunciation of the decisions adopted at the CMEA meeting of February issued by the Rumanian Plenum assembled early in March 1963 was hardly a

40 The most comprehensive and authoritative statement is Gheorghiu-Dej's, *ibid.*, December 30, 1962.
41 *Ibid.*, December 30, 1962.

spontaneous action motivated by frustration over rejection of the Rumanian positions in Moscow.[42] The Rumanians, having agreed to take a formal stand against Russian domination of the bloc and Soviet restrictions on Rumania's independence, had actually been readying themselves for a showdown since November.[43]

During the winter of 1962–1963 the Rumanian leadership had intensified its drive to rally the masses for a common national, and essentially anti-Russian, effort. A sweeping amnesty to political prisoners was granted concurrently with the pursuit of a massive campaign for strengthening the "socialist patriotic" sentiments of the population at large in support of the party's programs.[44] At the same time, Gheorghiu-Dej and his associates—clearly encouraged by the repeated Sino-Soviet confrontations at the Italian, Czechoslovak, and East German party congresses—were consciously veering toward a position of potential mediators of the Sino-Soviet conflict, champions of the unity of the socialist camp, and chief exponents and defenders of the principles of the Moscow Declaration of 1960. It is indeed noteworthy that at all these congresses Rumanian speakers carefully avoided all controversy. Even when denouncing the Albanian ideological "heresies" or criticizing directly or by implication Chinese support for the Albanian views, the Rumanians called for socialist reconciliation and unity in the spirit of the Moscow Declaration.[45] These appeals for peaceful resolution of ideological differences, cessation of polemics, and restoration of harmony may have resembled Khrushchev's; however, they bore an even more striking resemblance to the Rumanian "declaration of independence" of April 1964.

It remains a matter of conjecture what form the Rumanian course would have assumed had the Russians and their supporters agreed to the Rumanian formula for the CMEA at the Moscow meeting of February 1963. In all probability Gheorghiu-Dej would not have relinquished the trump cards and opportunities made available to him by the "objective international conditions" of the winter of 1962–1963. His deep-seated mistrust of Khrushchev, his long experience with Russian economic exploitation and inter-

---

[42] *Ibid.,* March 9, 1962.

[43] On these points see also Floyd, *Rumania,* pp. 70–99.

[44] A most interesting assessment of the amnesties and political attitude of the Rumanian population was made by the State Council at its meeting of April 5, 1963 (*Scînteia,* April 9, 1963).

[45] See footnotes 37, 38. *Scînteia,* January 19, 1963, published Chivu Stoica's speech at the East German Congress.

ference in Rumania's internal affairs, and, by now, his genuine pride in his regime's achievements in socialist construction were certainly contributing factors in his search for political as well as economic freedom. Thus, even if the Russians had agreed to his economic terms in February—as they did in July—the Rumanian course would most likely not have been altered to any significant degree. But the rejection of his demands provided Gheorghiu-Dej with an opportunity formally to assert the Rumanians' determination to be masters in their own house and a force to be reckoned with in international affairs, within and without the socialist camp.

It is highly significant that in the communiqué published at the end of the plenum of March 5–8 a broad political doctrine, transcending the immediate issues of international economic relations, was enunciated by the party's high command. Upon restamping its approval of the positions defended by Bîrlădeanu and invoking the validity of the "fundamental principles of the Socialist international division of labor" adopted by the CMEA in June 1962, the communiqué charged that not only these principles but also those of the 1960 Moscow Declaration proclaiming "observance of national independence and sovereignty, of full equality of rights, comradely mutual aid and mutual benefit" were violated.[46] The Moscow Declaration, as the repository of all rights of the members of the socialist camp, thus became the Magna Carta of the international Communist movement and the dagger as well as shield of the Rumanians. According to this interpretation the regime could justify in the name of the Declaration a series of distinctly anti-Russian actions initiated with the very purpose of asserting the strength and determination of the "new Rumania."

In retrospect, it has become evident that the Rumanian moves were designed not merely to force reconsideration by Russia and her supporters in CMEA of the decisions made in Moscow in February. Reconsideration was only one, and not necessarily the most important, goal. The plenum had merely approved the implementation of plans made earlier in anticipation of the Moscow resolution. It is known, for instance, that the negotiations with Italy which resulted in a major trade agreement in April were in progress in February. Nor were the discussions with Yugoslavia, leading to an agreement for joint construction of a colossal hydropower plant in the vicinity of the Iron Gates, or, for that matter, those with China ending in an improved commercial agreement,

46 *Ibid.*, March 9, 1963.

initiated by the plenum. However, the precipitous conclusion of these international understandings served the purpose of demonstrating to Russia and the international community at large that Rumania was pursuing policies dictated by its own national interests. This is not to say that certain other measures, clearly adopted only in March, and corollary statements by high Rumanian officials were not explicitly concerned with the assertion of independence from Russia as such or used for direct leverage against Moscow. The return of the Rumanian ambassador to Albania, acceleration of the drive for expanding trade with the West, and the constant reiteration of the principles enunciated by the plenum by men like Gheorghiu-Dej and Bodnăraş were evidently designed to seek concessions from Moscow but not at the price of abandonment of the Rumanian course.[47]

The Russians, reluctant either to take forceful steps against the recalcitrant Rumanians or to surrender to their demands, understandable as it was in the atmosphere after the Cuban crisis, merely played into the Rumanians' hands. The extended meeting of the CMEA's executive committee in April and the hurriedly convened extraordinary session of the same body held in Warsaw fifteen days later failed to resolve the differences between Rumania and the opposition, but compromises favorable to Bucharest were offered. Had the Rumanians been in a pliable mood, a basis for reconciliation might have been found in May when a special mission headed by Podgorny was dispatched to Bucharest for that very purpose.[48] It is true that the Russians did not meet all of the Rumanians' demands, but they did recognize the substantial achievements of Gheorghiu-Dej's regime and promised observance of the principles of the Moscow Declaration as interpreted by the Rumanians. But Gheorghiu-Dej, not satisfied with general statements of principle and in any case mistrustful of Moscow, insisted on formal acceptance of Rumania's rights to industrialize according to the party's own plans, rather than Khrushchev's or the CMEA's, and unconditional recognition by the Kremlin of the equality of all socialist countries and their right to determine their own destiny.[49] Gheorghiu-Dej's views, anticipatory of Maurer's formulation of Ru-

[47] Convenient summaries of these events may be found in Brown, "Rumania," op. cit., pp. 26–28, and J. B. Thompson, "Rumania's Struggle with Comecon," East Europe, Vol. XIII, No. 6 (June 1964), p. 7. See also Bodnăraş' May Day speech, Scînteia, May 2, 1963, and Gheorghiu-Dej's on the occasion of U Thant's visit to Rumania, ibid., May 7, 1963.

[48] Podgorny's principal statement is in ibid., June 5, 1963.

[49] Gheorghiu-Dej's principal statement is in ibid.

mania's role in the socialist camp issued in November and of the *Statement* of April 1964, were indicative of the breadth of the Rumanians' aspirations and apprehensions. In the spring of 1963 the principal aim of Gheorghiu-Dej and his associates was to prevent any Russian move, no matter in what field, that could restore the unity of the socialist camp and the Soviet bloc under exclusive Russian leadership and consequently threaten the Rumanian course and their own political careers. The principal strategy was exploitation of the Sino-Soviet conflict.

The exclusive publication within the bloc of the Chinese "25 Points," in June, was designed to intimidate Khrushchev by citing Chinese support for Rumanian resistance to Soviet pressures on economic integration. It was also intended to emphasize Rumania's neutrality through presentation of both points of view, the Russian and the Chinese. Similarly, Gheorghiu-Dej's subsequent absence from the extraordinary summit meeting of bloc leaders convened by Khrushchev in Berlin in July was not only an act of defiance ascribable to unresolved differences over the CMEA but also a gesture of disassociation from any anti-Chinese moves on the eve of the Russo-Chinese ideological conference. The effectiveness of these tactics soon became apparent: the concessions made by Moscow and her more reliable partners at the CMEA meeting held in July after the *de facto* collapse of the ideological conference were clearly motivated by apprehension over reinflammation of the dispute with Peking and Bucharest. It is also noteworthy that the Rumanians' support of the Russian position on the nuclear test ban treaty and criticism of the Chinese rejection thereof could not be accounted for by Moscow's consenting to the Rumanian demands on the CMEA. The Rumanians' action did not imply reconciliation with Moscow any more than it did *refroidissement* with Peking. The Rumanian stand was officially described as fully compatible with the country's independent course, with its role as a potential mediator of the Sino-Soviet conflict, and as a devoted supporter of the principles of the Moscow Declaration of 1960.[50] And it was recognized as such—for strategic considerations rather than belief in the Rumanians' altruism or integrity—by the direct protagonists themselves, Russia and China, as well as by interested Western observers.

It is true that the Russians were very suspicious of Rumania's

50 On these developments see Thompson, "Rumania's Struggle," *op. cit.*, pp. 7–8, and, for background, Stephen Fischer-Galati, ed., *Romania* (New York: Praeger, 1957), pp. 140–142.

intentions and the Rumanians of Russia's. Though Khrushchev's hand was stayed by fear of totally alienating Rumania at a time of increased strain in Sino-Soviet relations, he remained fundamentally opposed to Gheorghiu-Dej's independent course. Certainly the Russians would have exerted pressure on Rumania to bring her back in line had it not been for the Chinese issue. Khrushchev's repeated criticism of the Rumanians' obduracy and obstructionist policies, veiled as it was, was unmistakable and reflected Russian irritation with its former satellite. Nevertheless, Moscow took in stride the ever blunter assertion of the primacy of the Rumanian party in the conduct of domestic and foreign affairs and the minimizing of Russia's contribution to the development of socialism in Rumania. The Russians must have listened with discomfiture to Ceauşescu's speech on August 23 reiterating all the themes objectionable to Moscow, and must have read with scorn the Chinese statement of congratulations to Gheorghiu-Dej reiterating Peking's "fraternal support" for his anti-Russian positions.[51] But the possibility of retaliation became even more remote in September and October as the ranks of the opposition to Russian policies toward China were swelled by Communist parties other than the Rumanian.

As conclusively shown by William Griffith, the Russian plans for excommunication of the Chinese and their sympathizers from the socialist camp, which emerged clearly by September 1963, were frustrated by the opposition of several parties closer ideologically to Moscow than to Peking, including the Rumanian.[52] But unlike the Italian or British, for instance, the Rumanian Communists' opposition to Moscow's scheme was concerned not so much with the impact that a formal split would have had on the international Communist movement per se as with the disastrous consequences that polarization and restoration of Russian command over the members of the bloc would have had on the Rumanian leadership. Gheorghiu-Dej, Maurer, Ceauşescu, and Bîrlădeanu knew that in any case they were marked men in the fall of 1963 and that their reprieve, if not salvation, rested on refinement of the strategy of developing immunity from retaliation from Moscow through the deepening of their independent course and expansion of their ties with supporters and protectors of their interests. It was in this

[51] The evolution of the Soviet-Rumanian controversy was traced with varying degrees of accuracy by the Western press. The official Rumanian version is contained in Ceauşescu's speech, *Scînteia*, August 23, 1963, an unequivocal statement of Rumanian positions.
[52] William E. Griffith, *The Sino-Soviet Rift* (Cambridge, Mass.: The M.I.T. Press, 1964), pp. 182–230.

spirit that the Rumanians presented their ideological and political dicta first during the preliminary discussions with Moscow on the proposed excommunication of Peking and, more audaciously, after Khrushchev bowed to those internal and external pressures that favored further negotiation rather than drastic action.

The unequivocal formulation of the Rumanian position in domestic and international affairs was contained in Maurer's article "The Unshakable Foundation of the Unity of the International Communist Movement," which appeared in *Problems of Peace and Socialism* in November 1963.[53] In essence, the Rumanians condemned Chinese rigidity as much as Russia's (and China's) desire to "impose on other parties its line and decisions, to go over the head of the party leadership of one country or another, to appeal for a change in it, to support groups inside or outside the fraternal parties of other countries." The latter statement, identical with that made in the "Declaration of Independence" a few months later, was as much of a warning to the Kremlin against interference in Rumanian affairs as a preliminary indication of the Rumanians' later stated intention to mediate the Sino-Soviet conflict. That these were the Rumanians' desiderata was evident from Maurer's not-too-subtle indication of his country's intention to pursue its own independent "neutral" course in the Sino-Soviet dispute provided that the Russians recognized Rumania as a leading member of the socialist camp—in fact the leader of a "third force" in the world Communist movement—and, of course, her independence and right to work out her own socialist destiny. The alternative to the Kremlin's acceptance of Rumania's status was not spelled out as specifically; by intimation, however, Bucharest could move more to the left in the direction of China or to the right in the direction of the West. It is clear, however, that in November 1963 the Rumanians thought they had found the best way to handcuff Moscow and acted accordingly.

It is also clear that Moscow was less than enthusiastic over Maurer's pronunciamento and that its displeasure was shared by the more developed nations of the bloc—Poland, Czechoslovakia, Hungary, and East Germany. While caught in a strategic box and thus unable to retaliate against the "upstart," Khrushchev apparently devised a counterstrategy of his own. Unable to apply economic or political sanctions without incurring major risks, he eyed the possibility of cutting Rumania down to size by reopening the eternal

---

[53] The original Rumanian text "Temelia de neclintit a unității mișcării comuniste internaționale" appeared in *Scînteia*, November 4, 1963.

Pandora's box of national rivalries and related territorial revisionism should Rumania contemplate outright defection or move too far out of line.

The exact date and circumstances under which territorial revisionism became an issue in Russo-Rumanian relations are somewhat uncertain. It is known, however, that territorial questions were raised by both sides in March 1964 in connection with Rumania's attempted mediation of the Sino-Soviet conflict.[54] Moreover, the Chinese had publicly raised similar questions as early as March 1963,[55] and the Rumanians had intensified their domestic nationalist campaign in early winter 1963–1964 with allusions to the country's historic frontiers.[56] Whether the accelerated drive for increased international recognition and mass support for the party's independent policies that followed the issuance of Maurer's statement was motivated by the regime's desire to strengthen its defensive position toward Russia or its prestige in the international community at large and the socialist camp itself is still open to debate. It is noteworthy, however, that the first overt anti-Russian action, the closing of Russian cultural institutions in Bucharest, occurred shortly after publication of Maurer's article and was accompanied by similar "cultural" steps designed to whet the Rumanians' old-fashioned anti-Russian appetites. The "Romanization" of the alphabet and tentative nationalist revision of historical studies concerning Soviet-Rumanian relations could hardly have been justified in terms of international prestige alone. On the other hand, the unprecedented breaking of the Soviet bloc's voting unity at the United Nations when the Rumanians cast a dissenting vote on issues related to Latin America in November and the extended state visit by Rumanian leaders to Yugoslavia during that same month could be regarded primarily as manifestations of Rumanian independence, as actions designed to improve the country's international posture.[57]

It is evident, however, that the Rumanian leadership was apprehensive about Russian pressures exerted in connection with the Sino-Soviet dispute throughout the winter of 1963–1964 and that the celebrated "mission to Peking" decided on in February 1964

---

[54] See pp. 101–102.

[55] Griffith, *The Sino-Soviet Rift,* pp. 110–111.

[56] This trend becomes evident from reading the specialized historical literature published during those months, particularly the articles and reviews appearing in *Studii.*

[57] On these points consult also Floyd, *Rumania,* pp. 89–96.

was a defensive rather than an offensive move. The recapitulation of the immediate circumstances contained in the *Statement* of April 1964 and the ensuing commentary on matters related to the mission leave no doubt as to the Rumanians' motivations.[58] Moscow's decision of early February to bring matters to a head with Peking and to secure compliance with its plans from members of the bloc moved the Rumanians to seek postponement of the showdown pending mediation by Bucharest. That both the Russians and Chinese accepted the Rumanians as "honest brokers" for their own tactical reasons only has been conclusively demonstrated by Griffith.[59] That the Rumanians shared the Russian and Chinese skepticism and cynicism is also unquestionable. The mission headed by Maurer and comprising Bodnăraş, Ceauşescu, and Stoica had only one aim: to avert a formal break between Russia and China that could lead to the restoration of Russian domination over the bloc and at least severe curtailment of Rumania's independence. The Rumanians, in February 1964, knew that a viable third force in the international Communist movement could not be established under their leadership; however, they had some expectation that a stalemate could be secured that would give Bucharest enough time to strengthen its position in the socialist camp and the international community in general. The Rumanians were not lulled into complacency and false hopes. Because of the inauspicious circumstances for a successful mission, they had readied political alternatives in the likely event of failure. From as early as February, the Rumanian leaders sought to consolidate their ties with the Rumanian people and the West. The appearance of the principal members of the power elite at various local and regional party meetings that month, during which they extolled the virtues and correctness of the party's policies, coincided with the massive liberation of political prisoners and intensification of economic and cultural contacts with the West. Still, Gheorghiu-Dej and his associates did not want to accept the Rumanian people and the West, both anti-Communist,

---

58 *Declaraţie cu privire la poziţia Partidului Muncitoresc Romîn în problemele mişcării comuniste şi muncitoreşti internationale adoptată de Plenara lărgită a C.C. al P.M.R. din aprilie 1964* [Statement on the Stand of the Rumanian Workers' Party Concerning the Problems of the International Communist and Working-Class Movement Adopted by the Enlarged Plenum of the Central Committee of the RWP Held in April 1964] (Bucharest: Editura Politică, 1964), pp. 9–14 (hereafter cited as *Declaraţie*). Revised English translation: William E. Griffith, *Sino-Soviet Relations, 1964–1965* (Cambridge, Mass.: The M.I.T. Press, 1967), pp. 269–296.

59 Griffith, *Sino-Soviet Relations, 1964–1965*, pp. 31–34, with ample bibliographical references.

as the mainstays of a policy of independence from Russia as long as the unity of the socialist camp could be preserved at least *pro forma* and economic and political sanctions by Moscow could be averted by action *en famille*. The failure of the mission to China, however, forced reconsideration and issuance of a formal declaration of independence shortly after the delegation's return from Peking, via Moscow.

It is now believed that the publication of the *Statement* in April 1964 was prompted by Khrushchev's determination to seek the expulsion of the Chinese from the international Communist movement following the *de facto* rejection of the Rumanian proposals by the Chinese and the consequent rejection by Moscow of Rumania's self-appointed role of mediator and maverick in the bloc.[60] From what is known of the negotiations in Peking and the subsequent Soviet-Rumanian discussions in Moscow, Maurer and his companions returned empty-handed from both capitals. But whereas Peking sought to encourage the Rumanians' independent course despite the inadmissibility of their proposals, Moscow sought to force the unsuccessful Rumanians back into line. Upon the Rumanians' admission of failure it is reported that Khrushchev formally (but not publicly) raised the disturbing question of territorial revisionism in Transylvania. Whether the listing of territorial adjustments in Asiatic Russia as part of the Chinese price for moderation in the dispute with Moscow was used by the Chinese and the Rumanians for tactical purposes or whether this represented a joint plea for territorial concessions by Moscow is not entirely clear. In the case of the Rumanians at least, it is probable that the Chinese demands for Soviet territories were linked with the Rumanian aspirations to Bessarabia only to the extent of impressing Khrushchev with the existence of this common Sino-Rumanian bond. The restitution of Bessarabia was not yet regarded as the price for Rumanian neutrality and basic adherence to Khrushchev's positions in international affairs. Khrushchev, however, sought to take advantage of the Rumanians' failure to reassert his waning authority in Rumania by suggesting the holding of plebiscites in all areas of the Communist world where territorial questions could be raised. In Rumania's case he specifically indicated his readiness to allow such plebiscites in Bessarabia as well as in Transylvania. The thinly veiled threat of reopening the Transylvanian question coupled with the decision to bring all aspects of the Sino-Soviet dispute into the

60 On these points consult *Declaraţie*, pp. 5–61. Compare the author's interpretation with Floyd, *Rumania*, pp. 100–117.

open forced the Rumanians to act. Aware that the majority of the members of the Soviet bloc supported Moscow in its conflict with Peking and its disagreements with Bucharest, Gheorghiu-Dej and his associates were faced with an undesirable set of alternatives. In April 1964, as the Sino-Soviet polemics which Bucharest sought to end flared up more fiercely than ever, the Rumanian party's Central Committee met in a lengthy enlarged plenum to charter a safe course. Unable to rely on Peking economically and in any case unsympathetic toward Chinese ideological extremism, and fearful of Russian pressures, the Rumanians decided to secure their independence by issuing a statement of positions that would embarrass Moscow, preclude retaliatory action by Khrushchev, and obtain Western economic and political support against the Kremlin. The concept of the independent, "neutral," socialist nation, devoted to peaceful coexistence as well as to the unity of the socialist camp, emerged unmistakably, but not voluntarily, in April 1964.

In essence, the *Statement on the Stand of the Rumanian Workers' Party Concerning the Problems of the World Communist and Working-Class Movement* represented only a reformulation of standard Rumanian political themes. Its significance lay in making public what had been known by the initiated at home and abroad, in airing the party's grievances and aspirations, in formally revealing the Rumanians' intentions to attain their goals by all means compatible with the maintenance of their independence and sovereign rights. Indeed, the most important part of the *Statement* was not the thinly veiled attack on traditional Russian interference in Rumanian affairs but the unequivocal declaration that the right of all nations, whether large or small, whether members of the socialist camp or not, solely to determine their national destiny on the basis of specific national conditions had to be internationally guaranteed. However, even if in April 1964 the Rumanian Communists were particularly anxious to secure such guarantees from all opposed to Russian domination of Rumania, particularly China and the United States, their ultimate concern was to maintain control in Rumania proper. The doctrine of Rumania for the Rumanians, for the socialist camp, for the international community in general, for peace, for equalitarianism, for the national liberation movement, for everybody and everything—all contained in the *Statement* —meant, in the final analysis, Rumania for the Rumanian Workers' Party. On April 22, 1964, Gheorghiu-Dej declared his own and his party's independence at a time when his own and his associates' future was in greater jeopardy than that of his country. The unequivocal and exclusive identification of the party with Rumania was both premature and unrealistic. The implementation of the principles of the declaration of independence depended on careful exploitation of internal and external contingencies. In the spring of 1964 the Rumanian leaders chartered a course that was to prove more dangerous than expected.

CHAPTER FIVE

THE LEGACY OF GHEORGHIU-DEJ

It was not by coincidence that Rumania's first major political move after the issuance of the *Statement* was to dispatch a top-level delegation to Washington. Though the overt purpose of the envoys, headed by the chief of the State Planning Commission, Gheorghe Gaston-Marin, was to strengthen Rumania's economic and cultural ties with the United States, it is clear that the Rumanians were also seeking assurances against possible retaliation by Moscow. The mission to Washington was so interpreted by Moscow and by the people of Rumania. Its anti-Russian nature was only thinly disguised by the Rumanian leaders' classification of the visit as a manifestation of Rumania's independence in conformity with the principles enunciated in April 1964.[1]

It is now known that the dramatic *rapprochement* with the United States did not receive unqualified endorsement by the party leadership. There were serious misgivings about the reliability of the United States as a potential protector of Rumania's interests, in view of the inevitable antagonizing of the Soviet Union. Doubts were also expressed about the possible consequences of increased exposure of the masses to Western "bourgeois" influences and political reliance on Rumanian nationalism with distinct anti-Russian overtones. The decision to seek assistance from the most powerful nation in the West on the assumption that Russian fear of the United States and American material aid would ensure the Rumanians the best of three worlds was Gheorghiu-Dej's, Maurer's, and Gaston-Marin's, and as such received the support of the more circumspect Ceaușescu, Bîrlădeanu, Stoica, and Bodnăraș. It is not certain whether any serious objections to the *rapprochement* with the United States were voiced by these men during the April plenum and the following meetings of the highest party echelons, but

---

1 Wide publicity was given in the Rumanian press to the visit of the delegation in late May and early June. See *Scînteia*, May 21, June 2, 1964.

the assumption of extreme nationalist and anti-Russian positions was subject to extensive discussion.[2]

However, nothing succeeds like success, and in May Gheorghiu-Dej appeared confident that his policies would prevail. The talks between Gaston-Marin's and Averell Harriman's teams did not bring spectacular results. But Bucharest secured the promise of increased American economic activity and technological assistance, and Gaston-Marin left with the conviction that the United States would not attempt to influence the political order in Rumania and probably would even bail out the Rumanian Communist regime in the event of a showdown with Russia.[3] He therefore reinforced Gheorghiu-Dej's determination to obtain the maximum concession from Moscow—unequivocal recognition of Rumania's independence.

The American crutch was judged essential by Gheorghiu-Dej. The Russians had indeed tried to intimidate the Rumanians as soon as the decision to send Gaston-Marin to the United States was made public, by denouncing the Rumanian action as contrary to the interests of the camp and the principles of the CMEA.[4] A hastily organized delegation sent to Moscow to explain the Rumanian course late in May was badly received and failed to iron out existing differences.[5] Toughened by the successful negotiations with the United States, the Rumanian leadership then decided that the best defense was indeed the best offense. It pushed its advantage by seeking further anchors in the West but without neglecting the opportunities provided by Khrushchev's renewed resolution to put the Communist house in order by expelling the Chinese from the socialist community of nations. If the Rumanian game, as it unfolded in the spring and early summer, appeared extremely risky to startled Western observers and even to Tito, who personally warned Gheorghiu-Dej of the dangers of provoking Khrushchev, it did not prevent Gheorghiu's team from playing it to win.[6] In June the Rumanian leadership went to the people to explain the signifi-

[2] Gaston-Marin's demotion in July 1965 was clearly connected with his pro-American orientation and ascendancy in the Rumanian party; it was a result of his swaying Gheorghiu-Dej toward a pro-American policy. See pp. 110–112, 114–116.

[3] Summary of the principal provisions and outstanding issues in *The New York Times*, May 27, 31, 1964.

[4] Radio talk by Boris Tarasov, "The Cooperation of Equals," broadcast over Radio Moscow on May 18, 1964; also *The New York Times*, June 9, 1964.

[5] *Pravda*, May 26, 1964.

[6] *The New York Times*, June 26, 1964.

cance and implications of the *Statement*. Exuberantly, Gheorghiu-Dej and those speaking on his behalf launched into unprecedented fulminations against traditional Russian interference in Rumanian internal affairs in an effort to seek total identification of the interests of the masses and the party in the common bond of anti-Russian nationalism. Whether the slogan of "Socialist Rumania for the Rumanians" was as acceptable as "Rumania for the Rumanians" had been in pre-Communist days is uncertain; but the response of the population at large was extremely favorable to the new Rumanian line. The emptying of jails of political prisoners and the reinstatement of these men in the new Rumania, the unrestricted opening of the country to Western tourists as well as to friends and relatives of the now-integrated class enemy, the rapid reintroduction of Western cultural productions and even newspapers, and, above all, the publicizing of Rumania's commitment to develop further her ties with the West inevitably raised the Rumanians' hopes for a freer and better life.[7] And even if the people took their leaders' new nationalism, professions, and promises *cum grano salis,* they were encouraged by the belief that a return to Stalinism was virtually barred by the dispute with Russia and reliance on the West.

It remains a matter of conjecture whether the "liberalization" of political and cultural life was motivated primarily by pragmatic political considerations or whether it reflected the rising influence of the younger party cadres and the professional groups who had become indispensable for the successful construction of socialism in Rumania. Whereas this question remains unresolved to this day, it would appear that in the spring of 1964 the determining factor in all major decisions remained the threat of Russian pressure if not direct intervention. It is indeed noteworthy that at least until August 23 the Rumanians maintained the utmost vigilance toward an irate but, hopefully, impotent Russia while pursuing policies distinctly counter to Russian interests. Typical of the Soviet-Rumanian game of cat and mouse was the unheralded but crucial visit to Moscow of a top-level Rumanian delegation, headed by Maurer himself, early in July.[8] It is now known that the trip was prompted by Khrushchev's decision of June 15 to summon an international Communist meeting to deal with the Chinese heresy.[9] Alarmed

---

[7] For a good summary of these developments, see *ibid.,* June 15, 1964.

[8] For details of the discussions see *ibid.,* July 15, 1964. For Rumanian comments see *Scînteia,* July 15, 1964.

[9] On these points see William E. Griffith, *Sino-Soviet Relations, 1964–1965* (Cambridge, Mass.: The M.I.T. Press, 1967), p. 42.

over the consequences that a Sino-Soviet showdown would have for Rumanian independence, the party decided to appease the Kremlin and concurrently to strengthen its ties with both the West and China. Maurer was to visit Moscow and preach the need for reconciliation of Sino-Soviet differences for the sake of unity of the socialist camp. But he was also to visit Paris in the spirit of peaceful coexistence and in search of economic and political advantages.

Details of Maurer's visit to Moscow are not available, but it is believed that the Russians sought to trade consent for the Rumanian independent economic course for Bucharest's support of Khrushchev's views on international Communist affairs. It is not known whether the threat of reviving the territorial questions related to Bessarabia and Transylvania was used by Moscow to secure Rumanian adherence to the Kremlin's formula for Russo-Rumanian reconciliation. But territorial revisionism was one of the major issues discussed perhaps even before Mao Tse-tung's deliberate injection of the Bessarabian issue in his celebrated anti-Russian statement made on July 10 while Maurer was still in Moscow.[10] Though it is improbable that Maurer would have provoked the Russians by bringing up that question directly, it is likely that Mao's statement did not take the Rumanians by surprise. In fact, some believe that the Rumanians held out the possibility of supporting the Russian position vis-à-vis China in return for consent to the eventual restitution of Bessarabia. Others are of the opinion that the Rumanians tried to persuade Khrushchev to reconsider the price for peace in the socialist world, to allow Bucharest to renew its mediation effort, and, in case of success, to reward the Rumanians for their good offices with Bessarabia. Be this as it may, the Rumanians apparently obtained Russia's reluctant consent to pursue their neutral course in the Sino-Soviet dispute and their hitherto frowned-upon policies toward the West. The territorial questions as well as those related to the CMEA were left in abeyance. Maurer's team left Moscow on July 14 with the growing conviction that the principles of the *Statement* of April 1964 had been *de facto* accepted by the Kremlin.[11]

Gheorghiu-Dej and his closest associates, however, remained mistrustful of Moscow. Maurer had returned from Paris early in August with promises of increased economic and cultural cooperation and, significantly, de Gaulle's recognition of the validity of the

10 *Ibid.*, pp. 28–30.
11 See footnote 8.

Rumanian course, so similar to his own vis-à-vis the United States.[12] But Maurer also realized that France alone could not provide decisive leverage against Russian pressures and that ultimately Rumania would have to work out its problems within the family of socialist nations, with the assistance of the West headed by the United States. That a compromise formula based on a careful review of the international situation and Maurer's recommendations was adopted by August 23 was amply proved by the events related to the twentieth anniversary of Rumania's liberation. By that time the Rumanian leadership had decided to emphasize its role of champion of the unity of the socialist camp and to avoid any further friction with Moscow. This was clearly the safest course at a time when Khrushchev continued to insist on holding the showdown conference on China and the United States seemed determined to intervene more actively in the Vietnamese conflict following the Tonkin Gulf incident.[13]

It is noteworthy that the Russians tried to exploit the Rumanian dilemma of relying concurrently on the "American aggressor" and on China. Mikoyan, sent to Bucharest on August 23, restated Russia's traditional friendship for Rumania and the community of Soviet-Rumanian interests while violently attacking American aggression in Vietnam.[14] At the same time Malinovsky, in a lengthy article in *Pravda,* gave the lie to the Rumanians' interpretation of their liberation by restating Russia's paramount role in August 1944 and in the subsequent construction of socialism in Rumania.[15] The Russians, however, proffered an olive branch to the Rumanians by assuring them of full adherence to the principles of the *Statement* of 1964 and the Moscow Declarations of 1957 and 1960, provided that Gheorghiu-Dej would not rock the boat of socialist unity through unwise commitments to the United States and China. It is also noteworthy that the Chinese sought to encourage Rumanian resistance to Russian pressure by contradicting the very arguments advanced by Mikoyan and Malinovsky. In Peking's interpretation of the *Statement,* the unity of a socialist camp of equals was a common Rumanian-Chinese position. Moreover, the "victors' rights"

12 For extensive press coverage see *Scînteia,* July 28–August 5, 1964. Text of the Franco-Rumanian communiqué: *Le Monde,* August 3, 1964.

13 See *Scînteia* article on Tonkin Gulf incident and its implications for Rumanian policies, August 10, 1964.

14 All official speeches in *Scînteia,* August 23–24, 1964.

15 R. Malinovsky, "On the Twentieth Anniversary of the Routing of the Hitlerites in the Iaşi-Kishinev Operation: A Glorious Victory," *Pravda,* August 20, 1964.

gained by the Rumanian people under the leadership of the Rumanian party in 1944 comprised the entire national historic legacy, lost territories and all. The Chinese, and their Vietnamese and Korean supporters, desisted in this context from condemning American imperialism and aggression in Vietnam; for Peking's purposes Rumania's flirtation with the United States was a price worth paying for her neutrality and, as such, support for the Chinese position in the Sino-Soviet conflict.

The Rumanian leaders, making allowances for their country's proximity to Russia and for China's and America's geographic and ideological remoteness, adopted a remarkably conservative position in expressing their views on the significance of Rumania's liberation and the lessons to be derived from that event. Far from announcing any spectacular new measures designed to strengthen the Rumanians' allegiance to the national Communist regime or to spell out in greater detail the character, achievements, and plans of independent Rumania, Gheorghiu-Dej merely summarized the *Statement* of April 1964.[16] The *Statement* had become the fundamental doctrinal pronunciamento and needed no reinterpretation. It provided the optimum scope for tactical adjustments and maximum flexibility in times of political uncertainty. Further Rumanian moves toward becoming more independent from Russia, a third force in the international Communist movement, and a major link between East and West appeared to have been arrested.

Gheorghiu-Dej's caution soon became less evident when, in the fall, "objective international conditions" seemed to shift in his favor. Khrushchev's downfall in October provided opportunities that were not to be missed by the Rumanians. In the period of adjustment Brezhnev and Kosygin were judged more vulnerable than the deposed leader and hence more likely to condone, if not to ratify, the consolidation of Rumania's independent course. The Russian attempt to reconcile differences with China and the related postponement of the international Communist meeting whetted Gheorghiu-Dej's appetite. By December he was ready to reassert himself as the champion of arbitration and to state the price for his good offices in placing Bessarabia on the trading block of the socialist camp. It would be erroneous to assume that the publica-

---

[16] Principal statement by Gheorghe Gheorghiu-Dej, *A XX-a aniversare a eliberării Romîniei de sub jugul fascist* [The Twentieth Anniversary of the Liberation of Rumania from the Fascist Yoke] (Bucharest: Editura Politică, 1964), pp. 5–30.

tion early in December of the seemingly innocuous historic study "Karl Marx's Notes on the Rumanians" was intended to reinforce the socialist patriotism of the masses.[17] Little was to be gained by appealing to "bourgeois nationalist" passions at a time when the Rumanian people had lost most of the interest they may once have had in the reacquisition of Bessarabia. The utilization of Marx as a spokesman for Rumanian rights to that province and the related condemnation of Russian imperialism were intended to lodge a valid "socialist" claim, which was to be resolved concurrently with similar socialist (Chinese) irredenta. It is doubtful that Gheorghiu-Dej was counting on a reconciliation between Russia and China or the possibility of Russia ever returning Bessarabia. But once the Rumanian claims were raised, he could always renounce them in return for Russian concessions elsewhere. This, in fact, appears to have been his strategy, for during the same month of December his regime renewed the drive to expand economic and political ties with the West.

The Rumanian decision to intensify the process of "building bridges" to France and the United States, formally made at the meeting of the Central Committee of November 30–December 1, was based on the belief that the new Soviet leaders had no choice but to tolerate Rumania's independent policies. It was also based on the assumption that the United States, following the election of Lyndon B. Johnson as President, would continue to build its own bridges to Eastern Europe and refrain from escalating the Vietnamese conflict. The latter assumption was questioned by certain members of the Central Committee, who frowned on Gheorghiu-Dej's pro-American policies. Bîrlădeanu, in particular, is known to have advocated closer ties with France, a country whose positions vis-à-vis China and Vietnam were more compatible with Rumania's. Gaston-Marin, on the other hand, was the most explicit champion of implementation of the agreements reached in Washington in June and apparently persuaded Gheorghiu-Dej of the advantages of dealing with the world's leading power. In characteristic fashion it was agreed to negotiate concurrently with both France and the United States.[18]

The political character of these allegedly economic and cultural

---

17 A. Oţetea and S. Schwann, eds., *K. Marx-Insemnări despre români* (Bucharest: Editura Academiei, 1964).

18 See Gheorghiu-Dej's speech to the National Council of the People's Democratic Front, *Scînteia*, December 25, 1964, and Maurer's to the Grand National Assembly, *ibid.*, December 27, 1964. Also *The New York Times*, January 5, 1965.

THE LEGACY OF GHEORGHIU-DEJ   111

negotiations was so evident that for the first time it was officially publicized as such. Maurer stated that much in his year-end speech to the Grand National Assembly reviewing the progress of socialist construction. Bîrlădeanu admitted unequivocally on the occasion of Giscard d'Estaing's state visit to Bucharest for the signing of a long-range Franco-Rumanian agreement in February 1965 that the political importance of that agreement clearly exceeded its economic significance. The pro-American wing also outdid itself first by suggesting the establishment of joint American-Rumanian companies and later by publicizing the initialing of agreements between the Rumanian government and the Firestone Tire and Rubber Company and the Universal Oil Products Corporation. In early February 1965 the regime believed that it was about to wrest the maximum benefits from both the capitalist and Communist worlds. Relations with France and the United States had never been better. And even if the oft-delayed meeting of Communist parties to consider the Sino-Soviet dispute was to convene in March, it appeared safe to reject Moscow's invitation at a time when Khrushchev's successors were desperately trying to avoid a formal split in the socialist camp. The confident Rumanian leadership decided to trumpet to the Rumanian electorate its successes and the inevitable triumph of its time-proved policies that transformed Rumania into a socialist dream nation. The emphasis at the forthcoming elections to the Grand National Assembly, scheduled for March 7, was to be placed on the attainment of the country's historic goal: a prosperous socialist Rumania.[19] But at that very moment the roof of the house that Gheorgiu-Dej built began to cave in.

Two separate factors, one internal and the other external, were to mark the end of an era: Gheorghiu-Dej's incurable illness, which brought death one month later, and America's determination to engage in direct military action in Vietnam at the risk of burning its bridges to Eastern Europe. To what extent the decision to mend Rumania's fences with Moscow was Gheorghiu-Dej's own or that of his heir apparent Ceaușescu is unknown. But it is clear that the dispatching of Gaston-Marin to Moscow for talks on Soviet-Rumanian economic cooperation for the period 1966–1970 reflected the need for accommodation with the Soviet Union at a time of major uncertainty. The Soviet-Rumanian trade protocol concluded on February 17 eased the strains between Bucharest and Moscow

[19] The height of Rumanian optimism was reached early in February 1965 and was still evident during the electoral campaign. See *Scînteia,* particularly the February 8–March 8, 1965 issues.

and provided the Rumanians with an agreement essentially compatible with the oft-repeated principles of the *Statement* of April 1964. Nevertheless, the mission to Moscow represented a clear setback for Gheorghiu-Dej's and Gaston-Marin's plans for socialist construction with American assistance. This *bouleversement* became more serious as American involvement in Vietnam assumed greater proportions. On March 5 Gheorghiu-Dej, who had carefully avoided any public condemnation of American policies, at last came to grips with his dilemma; but the denunciation of Washington and support of Ho Chi Minh's war of liberation was a choice he would have preferred to avoid.[20] A change in tactics had become necessary, however, not only because of the Vietnamese crisis as such but also because of the possibility of a Sino-Soviet *rapprochement* at a time of "imperialist aggression" against a key member of the socialist camp. Gheorghiu-Dej died on March 19; Nicolae Ceauşescu succeeded him on that very day.

Ceauşescu's succession had been taken for granted by the majority of the Rumanian population, but the manner of man he was was known only to the initiated.[21] Whether the character of his rule and the nature of his policies would have been different had he come to power under more auspicious international circumstances is a matter of speculation. It soon became apparent, however, that both his style and intentions were substantially different from his predecessor's. Even before the Vietnamese conflict reached the scale of an undeclared American–North Vietnamese war and the Firestone Tire and Rubber Company terminated its negotiations with the Rumanian government, thus even before it became clear that the United States had assigned a much higher priority to Southeast Asia than to Eastern Europe, Ceauşescu was moving deftly in the direction of taking the Rumanian independent course outside the daily fluctuations of international power politics. While clearly aware of the tactical advantages to be derived from the exploitation of the Sino-Soviet rivalry or the growing differences in Chinese and Russian policies toward Vietnam and the United States, Ceauşescu sought first to consolidate and legalize the historic achievements of the Rumanian Workers' Party as symbolized by the Rumanian independent course. The principles contained in the *Statement* of April 1964 were to be translated into political theory and practice

20 Gheorghiu-Dej's far-reaching speech in *ibid.*, March 6, 1965.
21 A brief biographical sketch of Ceauşescu may be found in J. F. Brown, *The New Eastern Europe* (New York: Praeger, 1966), pp. 282–284.

at a higher level than a mere declaration by a plenum of the Central Committee. They were to be ratified and expanded first by the Fourth Congress of the Rumanian party, hastily summoned for July, and more lastingly by a new constitution, the ultimate recorder of continuity and change in the process of construction of a Socialist Rumania. Thus, in Ceauşescu's view and that of his *hommes de confiance,* the legacy of Gheorghiu-Dej was the establishment of an independent Socialist Rumania on the merits of actual achievements rather than of fishing in troubled international waters. This inward, national orientation reflected the highest commitment to national communism per se as well as to the validity of the gains realized under Gheorghiu-Dej's leadership. It did not, however, represent approval for the deceased leader's methods and compromises with Marxist-Leninist doctrine.

The view that Rumania could and should stand on its own Communist feet and principles was expressed first in the funeral oration at Gheorghiu-Dej's grave.[22] It was restated more explicitly and forcefully at the Plenum of the Central Committee of April 14–15 when both the date of the congress, July 19, and the agenda were made public.[23] It became even more evident during the several meetings of the party leadership with regional party committees and men of science and letters, whose support for the consolidation of a "democratic" socialist Rumania Ceauşescu avidly sought.[24] It was unmistakable by June, when the name of the party was changed to Communist, when admission requirements were liberalized "to reflect the present stage of development of our society," and when the draft of the new constitution announced the country's new name, "The Socialist Republic of Rumania."[25] This new, forceful orientation was also underlined by forthright pursuit of independent foreign policies truly consistent with the principles of the *Statement* of April 1964. While not abandoning any of its fundamental positions, the regime refined and re-expressed them in terms of the national interest of a sovereign Communist state. What suited that interest and was consistent with the principles of the *Statement* was defended and promoted; crude political expediency was avoided. It may be argued that Ceauşescu had no alternative in view of the deterioration of the international situation in the spring

22 *Scînteia,* March 25, 1965.

23 The official interpretation of the decisions and their implications was made available in some detail by Chivu Stoica in a speech on the occasion of the celebration of Lenin's 95th birthday on April 21, 1965 (*ibid.,* April 22, 1965).

24 See Ceauşescu's speech to writers and artists, *ibid.,* May 20, 1965.

25 *Ibid.,* June 3, 29, 1965.

of 1965. Nevertheless, the general impression was conveyed to the international community and the Rumanian people that his regime was sincerely committed to the strengthening of Rumania's independence under principled Communist rule. And this impression was confirmed and strengthened during and after the party congress in July.

In an otherwise uneventful meeting, the Rumanian Communist Party restated its national orientation and its determination to pursue only such internal and foreign policies as were compatible with the national interest and well-being and, naturally, with the principles of Marxism-Leninism. Ceauşescu asserted his dedication to further strengthening Socialist Rumania and to enlisting the best available talent for that purpose.[26] Inside the party his policy meant consolidation of his own power through the packing of the Central Committee with his own men, mostly young Rumanians, and unequivocal assumption of the number one position in the hierarchy. Outside the party it meant extending the process of national and social reconciliation with the population at large. Officially at least, the "collective leadership" of Ceauşescu, Maurer, Stoica, Bodnăraş, Bîrlădeanu, Apostol, and Drăghici, and the rank and file of the Rumanian party and people were united in the pursuit of the goals as enunciated in April 1964 and as reinterpreted and reformulated at the congress of 1965.[27]

It is clear that the abandonment of certain aspects of Gheorghiu-Dej's legacy in 1965 was, however, involuntary. The renunciation of claims to Bessarabia, formally made by Ceauşescu during a visit to Moscow early in September, could be accounted for only in terms of political duress caused by loss of leverage during the Vietnamese war. The Russians' formal recognition of the validity of the principles of the congress and Rumania's independence was not considered a satisfactory *quid pro quo* by Bucharest.[28] In fact, the "Moscow concessions" reflected realization of the impasse caused on the one

26 Ceauşescu's views are clearly expressed in Nicolae Ceauşescu, *Raport la cel de al IX-lea congres al Partidului Comunist Român* [Report to the Ninth Congress of the Rumanian Communist Party] (Bucharest: Editura Politică, 1965), pp. 5–101, hereafter cited as Ceauşescu, *Raport*. It is noteworthy that shortly before the meeting of the congress the assembly was rebaptized the Ninth Congress of the Rumanian Communist Party from the originally scheduled Fourth Congress of the Rumanian Workers' Party to emphasize legitimacy, continuity, and change.

27 Proceedings of the Ninth Congress, *Scînteia*, July 20–24, 1965. Of particular significance is the "Resolution of the Ninth Congress of the Rumanian Communist Party," *ibid.*, July 24, 1965.

28 Final communiqué, *ibid.*, September 12, 1965.

hand by "American aggression" in Vietnam and on the other by the seemingly irrevocable divorcement of Russia and China and the resultant futility of all mediation efforts. However, the reopening of the Bessarabian question in the spring of 1966 at a time of growing Sino-Soviet tension and renewed Russian pressures for unequivocal Rumanian commitment to the Moscow line indicates that Ceauşescu accepted the part of Gheorghiu-Dej's legacy concerning Rumania's exploitation of the Sino-Soviet dispute.[29]

Nevertheless, Ceauşescu's Rumanian Communist state will not be the same as Gheorghiu-Dej's. Even if it had been possible to pursue the course laid down by Gheorghiu, it is doubtful that Ceauşescu would have adhered to his predecessor's blueprint. Gheorghiu-Dej, influenced by Maurer, Gaston-Marin, and, in terms of general Western orientation, even by Bîrlădeanu, was leaning more and more toward the West, and Gheorghiu-Dejism was becoming more closely identified with Titoism than Gomułkaism. Ceauşescu's concept of independence, clearly more nationalistic, doctrinaire, and provincial, certainly less a function of international relations, is reshaping, by choice as well as by necessity, that course in a manner quite different from the defunct leader's. Ceauşescu's "New Rumania" is the Rumania of a representative but all-powerful Rumanian Communist Party. The broadening of the basis of the party's membership through inclusion of an increasingly larger number of technocrats and intellectuals, as well as peasants, has strengthened the organization's identification with the

[29] The reasons for Ceauşescu's repudiation of the concessions made in September 1965 appear to be directly connected with Russian pressures regarding Transylvania and with a renewed Rumanian drive to gain greater independence from Moscow at a time judged propitious for seeking additional concessions. The renunciation of Rumanian claims to Bessarabia in September 1965 has been regarded as a *quid pro quo* for abandonment of Russian support of Hungarian demands for a voice in Transylvanian affairs if not the very reopening of the entire Transylvania question. More than any other factor, continuing Russian support of Hungarian positions prompted Ceauşescu's reassertion of Rumania's historic rights to both Transylvania and Bessarabia and denunciation of traditional Russian interference in Rumanian affairs in his speech of May 7, 1966. On the other hand, the restatement of Rumanian rights to the now-Russian territory concurrently with Rumania's opposition to Russian control over the Warsaw Pact is clearly a reformulation of the maximum Rumanian price for settlement with Moscow at a time of continuing Sino-Soviet conflicts and France's withdrawal from NATO. In any event, Ceauşescu's speech on the occasion of the forty-fifth anniversary of the establishment of the Rumanian Communist Party unequivocally reiterated the party's determination to resist all external pressures and pursue policies compatible with the historic legacy of Greater Rumania and the Rumanian party. The complete text of the speech appeared in *ibid.*, May 8, 1966.

Rumanian population at large. The rejuvenation of the party apparatus, the rendering of the principle of democratic centralism into a meaningful political process, and, perhaps most significantly, the reconciliation of all social and national groups in the construction of a sovereign, prosperous, and respected Rumania, albeit under the strict direction of the Communist Party, represents the quintessence of Ceauşescu's political philosophy.[30] Ceauşescu's "New Rumania" will not be as dependent on the West, on Russia, or on any other external power as Gheorghiu-Dej's. Nor is it to be a country subject to "bourgeois ideology," "revisionist" or "dogmatist" interpretations of Marxism-Leninism, or any other influences incompatible with Rumanian "objective conditions." These conditions are to be determined only by the party in terms of its own traditions, the national traditions, and the ultimate triumph of communism at home if not necessarily throughout the world.

The Rumanian course at present is less spectacular than in Gheorghiu-Dej's days. It represents a stage of consolidation of the gains achieved under Gheorghiu-Dej's leadership, the attainment of the major political goal of the Rumanian party—an independent Communist Rumania.[31] Gheorghiu-Dej was a contributor to the acceleration of the process of "desatellization," to the reorientation of Russian foreign policy, to exploitation of all "objective conditions" in intercamp and international relations. His exceptional political acumen, courage, and tenacity accounted not only for his own political survival during twenty turbulent years but also for the victory of communism in Rumania. But political opportunism, necessary in the difficult circumstances under which he had to operate, and unmistakable association with Stalinism and the days of unmitigated terror have tarnished his image among the younger

[30] Ceauşescu's political philosophy is conveniently summarized in his report to the Ninth Congress, particularly the section on the Rumanian Communist Party, and the speech of May 7, 1966, referred to earlier. Ceauşescu, *Raport*, pp. 63–92; *Scînteia*, May 8, 1966.

[31] Ceauşescu's widely publicized speech of May 7, 1966, particularly his criticism of military blocs and thinly veiled demand for the eventual dissolution of the Warsaw Pact, is basically only a restatement of positions contained in the *Statement* of April 1964. Evidently, the party's immediate and long-range goal remains the lessening of Russian domination in Eastern Europe and removal of any possibility of Soviet retaliation against an independence-oriented, often defiant, Rumania. Compare Ceauşescu's statements, published in *Scînteia* of May 8, 1966, with those contained in Chapter III of the *Statement* of April 1964, with Gheorghiu-Dej's speech on the occasion of August 23, 1964 (*Scînteia*, August 23, 1964), with Ceauşescu's previous remarks to the Ninth Congress (*ibid.*, July 20, 1965) and on the occasion of the Rumanian-Soviet Friendship Rally in Moscow (*ibid.*, September 11, 1965). See also footnote 29.

and more critical members of the party. His legacy is to be completed by sincere and devoted Communists committed to his goals but not necessarily his methods. The Socialist Republic of Rumania is the New Rumania. It is to be led by representatives of the new generation in a manner compatible with the principles of Marxism-Leninism and the country's historic tradition, whose executors the Communists believe themselves to be. The old fighters for the supreme national goal of a Communist Rumania and all those supporting (or condoning) that goal, regardless of social or national origin and past mistakes, are to be led by Ceauşescu in the further consolidation and strengthening of their fatherland. A non-Marxist synthesis? Perhaps. But one realistically conceived in terms of Rumania's geographic location, achievements, traditions, and the paramount interests of the Rumanian Communist Party.

A NOTE ON BIBLIOGRAPHIC REFERENCES

The student of Rumanian problems and developments since World War II must ultimately rely on official Rumanian publications. Once a frame of reference has been established and the art of reading contemporary documents mastered, the press, compendiums of laws, decrees, resolutions, official communiqués, historical articles, and statistical compilations provide invaluable insight into the workings of the Communist system and evolution of domestic and foreign policies and actions. The most valuable single sources are *Scînteia*, the daily newspaper of the Central Committee of the Rumanian Communist Party, available for the years 1944–1966, and the *Buletinul Oficial* (*Monitorul Oficial* prior to 1949), the official compendium of laws and decrees of the regime. However, inasmuch as the latter publication is not available to the public, the reader is referred to the briefer collection *Colecție de legi, decrete, hotărîri și decizii*, published since 1949 and containing similar materials. Since 1952 a companion publication comprising only ministerial decisions has been made available, *Colecția de hotărîri și dispoziții*. Excerpts from official publications, primarily speeches by major political figures, proceedings of party congresses, and major policy statements have been published separately since 1945. The principal compilations of this kind have been indicated in the footnotes. A more exhaustive list is contained in the bibliography of Ghita Ionescu, *Communism in Rumania 1944–1962* (London: Oxford University Press, 1964), pp. 358–359, and throughout the latest annotated bibliographic guide to Rumania, Stephen A. Fischer-Galati, *Rumania: A Bibliographic Guide* (Washington: The Library of Congress, 1963).

Official and semiofficial *interpretations de textes* are made available through specialized periodicals. The principal and most authoritative journals, generally published since 1948, are *Analele Institutului de Istorie a Partidului de pe lîngă C.C. al P.C.R.*, the organ of the party's historical institute; *Lupta de Clasă*, the theoretical and policy organ of the Central Committee of the Rumanian Communist Party; *Probleme Economice*, published by the Institute of Economic Research of the Rumanian Academy; and *Studii*, the journal of the section for historical studies of the Academy.

Primary sources other than Rumanian are very few and generally unreliable. Apart from *émigré* publications such as *România*, the

119

organ of the Rumanian National Committee in New York, which provide occasionally "political gossip" of interest, only major newspapers like *The New York Times, Neue Zürcher Zeitung, Pravda,* and *Le Monde* publish information valuable to the researcher. However, the Western press has noticed Rumania only after the "independent course" became evident around 1963.

The paucity of secondary sources may in part be explained by lack of interest in the nonsensational. The only serious modern study on pre-Communist Rumania, Henry Roberts, *Rumania: Political Problems of an Agrarian State* (New Haven: Yale University Press, 1951), has synthesized and reinterpreted everything of value and consequence for understanding the country's historic legacy and its relevance for the study of the Communist order. The student is therefore referred to the bibliography of Roberts' book, on pp. 381–399, for a critical evaluation of the literature. Monographic literature on Communist Rumania is scarce and generally polemical. Excluding such obvious work *à thèse* like Reuben H. Markham, *Rumania Under the Soviet Yoke* (Boston: Meador, 1949), the only comprehensive symposium prior to the appearance of Ionescu's *Communism in Rumania* is Stephen Fischer-Galati, ed., *Romania* (New York: Praeger, 1957). Articles by specialists on Rumanian affairs did appear periodically, primarily in the fifties, in compendiums like Stephen D. Kertesz, ed., *The Fate of East Central Europe* (Notre Dame: University of Notre Dame Press, 1956) or *East Central Europe and the World: Developments in the Post-Stalin Era* (Notre Dame: University of Notre Dame Press, 1962). Valuable discussions were also contained in works like Hugh Seton-Watson, *The East European Revolution* (New York: Praeger, 1956), but a major specialized study, Ionescu's, became available only after the "independent course" was unmistakably recognizable in 1964.

Paradoxically, Ionescu—one of the most serious and assiduous students of Rumanian affairs—had virtually completed his manuscript two years before publication, thus missing the full impact of the "new course" and the reinterpretation of the events of 1952–1962 which that course made evident. Addenda and corrigenda have been provided by other specialists since 1962 in article or monographic form as indicated in the footnotes of this book. These bibliographic references together with those contained in Roberts' *Rumania*, Fischer-Galati's *Rumania: A Bibliographic Guide*, and Ionescu's *Communism in Rumania*, pp. 357–367, will supply the reader with a list of the materials essential for the study and comprehension of contemporary Rumania.

INDEX